Don't cry life gets better

By

Ja'Neise Million

Table of Contents

Chapter 1

I am tired of my life and the way it is going. I thought the year 2003 was heading in the right direction for me. We are six months into the year, and I am still sending out my resume. I cannot understand why terrible things keep happening in my life. Every time I try to better my life, it just falls apart. I am a 20-something-year-old single mother to a handsome four-year-old little boy named Josh, living in Norcross, GA, in a roach-infested apartment. I have not been on a date in a while because I do not have time to deal with men's bullshit right now. My mama tells me I have a look on my face that makes men run the opposite way. I frown because its true; I am unhappy because I feel God does not hear my prayer. I have prayed for a change in my life since I was seventeen. I sigh, I am still struggling.

Sometimes I don't even enjoy attending church to hear the word because it upsets me. The church leaders in my church don't teach us how to overcome the wicked devices that come against us. They tell the congregation to stop believing in voodoo and witchcraft. If you believe in that nonsense, then it will affect you. I shake my head; they must have skipped Acts chapter eight in the Holy Bible. It is hard to keep your faith secure when you keep going through so much crap.

I wish God would have taken me instead of my grandmother. I want to end my life, but I am scared I will burn in hell, and that's not how I want to spend my eternal life. So, I am stuck on this earth to suffer until the day I die. I cried so much I don't think I have any more tears left. I became so frustrated with my life that I sliced the side of my arm to see how it felt to cut my wrists. That crap hurts so bad, I cried like a flash flood. I do not understand how in the hell people can deal with that kind of pain. I even bought a gun to make it easy and fast. Unfortunately, someone broke into my apartment and stole my gun along with the bullets. They even took one of my raggedy 13-inch TVs and homemade foil hanger antenna. I cannot get a break. Now I'm broke, busted, and disgusted, living day by day.

I sigh, I am patiently waiting for a recruiter to contact me with a great job offer. I currently work at The Burger Shop, which pays minimum wage. They could only give me 15 hours a week, which sucks. So, I thought about tricking on the side, but I have a son, and I do not want him growing up disrespecting women. Hell, I would sell drugs, but I do not want to get caught and be a nobody bitch in jail. That limits me from getting fast money. So, when I am not working, all I do is sit on my couch, better known as the "comfort zone," looking out my window and watching people in my ghetto-ass neighborhood tricking, fighting, and slanging. I cannot complain because they take care of their family the best way they can. Oh shit, my sister Sharon is pulling up in the parking lot. What the hell does she want?

Sharon is my half-sister; we have the same daddy but different mothers. My mother is half white and half Black. Ms. Water, my neighbor, calls her two-tone. Sharon's mother is Latin, and my younger half-sister, Jada's mama, is Black American. The donor called her brown sugar. That's all I know about my sister's mother. From what my mama said, the donor, whom my sister calls daddy, kept his baby mama undercover from the family. Who knows if my mama is telling the truth? My dad's family has so many deep-rooted secrets I lost count. Sharon knocked at my door; I sighed. Do I want to answer the door? No! But she knows I'm home; my beat-up Oldsmobile is a dead giveaway. I call my son downstairs, "Josh,"

He answers, "Yes, ma'am."

I say, "Come downstairs and get the door, please." He slowly walks downstairs with a grin to open the door for his auntie. She greets him at the door, "Hey, big guy, give me a hug," he hugs his auntie, smiling. "Okay, go back to what you were doing, little man." He walks back upstairs, and my sister turns toward me, frowning. "Could you please not look so damn evil? Try smiling more. Geesh! You make me not want to come in and chill with you. And why are you sitting in front of the window like an old lady being nosey as hell?"

I scoff, "Don't start with me; what do you want anyway?" She sat beside me on my couch, frowning, "Girl, you need a new couch," I rolled my eyes at Sharon, "Either buy me a new sofa or shut the hell up." She smirks, "That's not going to happen, anyway. I cleaned my closet and brought you two bags of clothes and shoes."

I frown, "I already got clothes."

Sharon gives me the evil eye, "I know you are going through a hard time, and you can't afford to buy nice clothes right now, so I'm giving you some of my designer clothes."

I mock her, "Oh, lucky me, just put them by the door,"

Sharon has an attitude, "How about you get up from that raggedy-ass couch and get the clothes out of my car yourself." I suck my teeth, get up from the couch, and put on my slides by the door. I ask, "Can you unlock your car, please?" I walk out the front door to go outside to get the bags of clothes out of Sharon's Lexus.

Lord, I want Sharon to go home and leave me alone! As always, my neighbor Gina is sitting on the front porch drinking a beer. She waves, "Hey, Shanel," I cut my eyes at her as I wave back. Oh Lord, she's walking toward the car and asks, "What are you doing?"

I reply in a spicy tone, "I am trying to mind my damn business, something you don't know how to do." Gina sipped her beer and said, "Girl, you are funny, I'm just asking if you were coming over tonight to play spades. Damon is going to be there." Her married eyes are glistening for a man she can't have. I grab the thick, large plastic bag of clothes from Sharon's trunk, slanging them to the ground, missing Gina's feet by an inch. I slammed the car trunk down so hard, giving Gina a dirty look, "Let me tell you something. I don't care about Damon; I'm not coming over to play spades. I scoff. But you can tell Damon to come and see his son, okay? Now, if you would excuse me, I have things to do." she shrugs her shoulders, "All right, your loss." I drag the heavy black plastic bags of clothes on the concrete, walking toward my townhouse. Sharon meets me at the door. "Girl, are you crazy? These are expensive designer clothes. You do not drag greatness on no damn concrete."

I reply with a calmly, "Whatever, just help me get the bags in the door, please." She helps me with the bags, and I sit them on the side of the door. I sigh, walking back to my couch by the window, a roach crawls on the ceiling. Sharon runs to the couch, "Girl, you need to get this place sprayed. This place is filthy." I give her the nasties look, trying to keep my fist from hitting her face, "Thanks for the clothes, Sharon. You can leave my damn house now."

She questions me, "Why are you so bitter, Shanel?"

I reply in a harsh tone, "I am not bitter. I'm just tired, Sharon, now will you please go home," She props herself on the couch, trying to get comfortable, "Maybe you need to go to church and lay your burdens down at the altar for Jesus to handle," I turn to my sister, "How about you get out my damn house!"

Sharon frowns, "See, that is why you struggle." I get up from the couch, sighing sharply, standing by the window. "Sharon, please, I do not want to hear anything you have to say about the church. I have prayed and prayed, went to church, and given my tithes faithfully, so do not be telling me that's why I'm struggling."

She gets up from the couch and hugs me, "You need to trust in God and have faith," I remove Sharon's arms from around my neck, screaming, "Get out of my townhouse!" Sharon is startled. She walks towards the couch to put on her shoes, fussing, "You need to go to church and purge yourself from all this bitterness you have in your heart!" I walk toward the door and open it, "Will you hurry up and leave now!" Sharon reached for her purse and walked out the door. She screamed, "Bye, Shanel," I slammed the door behind her, walking back to my torn-down couch crying.

I am so sick and tired of people telling me what I need to do. I have done everything. I feel blocked from my blessings. Everyone is getting blessed but me. Both of my sisters have brand-new cars and are living well while I am still going through hell. They are shacking up with men, but they are still getting blessed. I fight temptation every day while my sisters give in to temptation. What is wrong with that picture? What am I doing wrong, Lord? Help me to understand so I can repent, Lord.

Chapter 2

Josh walks downstairs to the kitchen, rubbing his tummy, "Mommy, are you going to cook dinner?" I fight my tears from pouring, "All we have is peanut butter and a little jelly," he frowns, "That's it, Mommy?"

I point in his direction, "Hey, at least you have something to eat, boy. Now sit at the table and be thankful." As I am making Josh a sandwich, there is a knock at the door. I mumble to myself; I hope this is not Sharon as I walk to the door, "Who is it?"

"It's me, Damon," I open the door with that look on my face that my mama talks about,

He says, "Damn, could you not look so evil when you open the door?" I rolled my eyes at Damon, "What do you want?"

He replies, "I came by to see my son,"

I smirked, being sarcastic, "How nice, come in. Josh, your daddy's here." He comes walking out of the kitchen with a sad look, "hey, Daddy,"

Damon glanced at me, confused, "What's the matter, little man?"

Josh hesitates to look in my direction, then whines to his daddy, "I'm hungry," he hugs Josh, glaring in my direction.

I frown at my son, "Josh, go sit in the kitchen." He walks away from his dad with his head down.

Damon asked, "You need money for food?"

I laugh, "How are you going to ask me a dumb question? You should be asking me how much I need?"

Damon sighs, "How much do you need?"

"How much you got?" Damon pulled out four rolls of cash from his pockets."

I shake my head, "I see you still letting the devil use you."

"Do you want the money or not?"

I flop down on my couch. Damon walks over and joins me on the couch, "What's wrong now?"

"I am tired of you slanging drugs. That is not a real job. You do not get benefits from selling drugs.

It would help if you found a job that offers medical and dental insurance for our son. I am tired of taking government assistants. So, until you make that happen, do not bring blood money into my house. I do not want our son to grow up thinking it's okay to make money selling drugs."

Damon gets up from the couch, walking toward the door, "I had a real job that didn't pay shit!

"Calm your voice down and stop cussing in my house. Your son is in the kitchen," Damon walks into the kitchen, "Son, go upstairs so your mom and I can talk,"

Josh begins whining, "Daddy, Mommy hasn't fixed my peanut butter sandwich yet," Damon glances at me, "Little man, as soon as your mother and I finish talking, I will get you something to eat." Damon watches his son walk upstairs before joining me on the couch, "Okay, back to our discussion; the devil is not using me. I'm trying my best to make money. Whether it's good or bad, it's money, dammit."

I sigh, "Killing people is the best you can do?"

"People do not die from smoking weed. Most Black men in the hood are in a damn fucking recession. I cannot get a job to pay me what I'm worth. In case you forgot, I do have responsibilities," said Damon.

I raised my voice, "And I don't, ugh! You are so full of yourself. I may not be living the way I want, but I am living, doing it the honest way!"

Damon rubs his temples in frustration, "Well, I am not you. I cannot be working any damn minimum-wage job. That's just not me." I get up from the couch and walk toward the front door, "Fine! Do not return to my townhouse with that temptation; I am trying to live right." He gets up from the couch and walks toward me, pointing his finger at me, "You think God is going to bless you? Hell, look how you are living; he does not care anything about you. If you want to be happy, you got to get your own blessing yourself."

I shake my head, "Wow! Do you hear how stupid you sound?" I shout as I open my front door, "Get out of my house, Damon!" He walks out of my house shaking his head, chuckling. I slammed my front door so hard the roaches were running for cover. I walked back into the kitchen with tears in my eyes. I cannot keep doing this, God; I need help. I wipe the tears on my shirt, make my son a peanut butter and jelly sandwich, and cut off the edges. I called for my son to come downstairs to eat his sandwich.

He responds, "Yes, ma'am," Josh slowly comes downstairs. I set his plate on the table as he walked into the kitchen, "Sit down and eat, baby." He frowned at his peanut butter and jelly sandwich as he sat at the table, "Mommy, is this all we are going to eat?" I sat at the table next to my son, "Stop complaining. At least you are eating."

Josh feels his bread. "Mommy, may I have something to drink because this bread is hard?"

I chuckle as I get up from the table, "You can have some water," he pouts, "Hey, I can put some sugar in it; you can have clear Kool-Aid, better known as sugar water." Josh sucks his teeth, "I know you didn't suck your teeth at me?"

He sadly apologizes to me, "Sorry, Mommy,"

I sigh, shaking my head, "It's okay. Now say your grace and eat your sandwich."

Josh mumbles, "Yes, ma'am," I watch my son say his grace. He picks up his sandwich. I think to myself. He does not deserve to live like this. My eyes are hurting with so much pain every time he bites into that dry sandwich. I get up from the table and walk to the bathroom to wipe away my tears. There is a knock at my door, and I sigh, "Lord, who is it now?" I walk out of the bathroom toward the front door, asking, "Who is it?"

"Gina!" I opened the door. Gina gave me The Burger Shop bag, "Here, don't ask, bye," I took the bag. Josh comes out of the kitchen smiling joyfully, "Yeah, Burger Shop!" I frown, "No!" Josh begins to whine, "Mommy, please, I'm hungry,"

"Then eat your sandwich," Josh starts crying, "I don't want this sandwich; I want Burger Shop," I scream, "Ugh!" I walked out of my door, two townhouses down, banging on Gina's door in anger. Damon opened Gina's door. I threw the Burger Shop bag in his face. "You bastard!"

"What is your damn problem, Shanel?"

I scream, "You are Damon!" he picks up the Burger Shop bag and hands it to Gina, "You mad because I bought my son something to eat?"

I shout, "He is eating!" Damon shouts, "A peanut butter…" I cut him off, "Forget you, Damon!" I walk toward my townhouse. I see the neighbors standing outside enjoying the free movie and talking amongst themselves. Damon runs after me, grabbing my arm. I shout, "Let me go!" I hear the male neighbors shouting, "Don't hit that woman!" Damon ignores the neighbors and yells, "No, listen to me! Josh is my son, too!" I pull away from Damon, "Oh really," Damon rubs his head, looking around. He calms down and sighs sharply, "You need to get over yourself. You are so blind. You need to pull the shells off your damn eyes. Look at the damn world for what it is. God sees all these homeless, hungry people struggling every day. Do you believe God is going to come out of the sky and give us money, houses, and food? Wake the hell up, Shanel!"

"No, you wake up. You are just trying to justify your wrongdoing." Damon chuckles, "What am I doing so wrong? Huh? I am trying to make money and care for my son".

"I am, too," Damon frowns at me, "So working at a fast-food restaurant serving cholesterol and high blood pressure every day isn't killing people?"

I screamed from the top of my lungs, "Shut up!"

Damon smirks, "No, let's put it out there. We are both slowly killing people to get paid."

I calm my voice down, "It's not the same thing," he laughs at me, "Yes, it is. You do it the proper way, and I do it the illegal way." I suck my teeth, walking away from Damon. He shouts, "Yeah, you can't handle that truth, can you?" I open my front door and slam it behind me. "Ugh! He irritates the hell out of me, always got to prove a point to make himself look intelligent, oh dumb ass." I walk in the kitchen. Josh ate his sandwich but left his glass of water on the table. I chuckled to myself and sat down in the kitchen. I calm myself down before calling my son, "Josh, baby, where are you?" He replies, "I'm watching TV in your room, Mommy." I walk upstairs to my bedroom; he is lying in my bed, chilling, watching cartoons. "It's time to take a bath."

"Yes, Mommy," I run his bathwater in bathroom. He goes to get his pajamas. "Okay, baby, go take a bath." I sat on the side of my bed, watching TV while Josh went into the bathroom to take a bath. I sigh, I can't watch TV. My spirit is not at ease. I cannot pray, and I don't have anybody to talk to now. My mama is too busy doing her own thing; she could care less about me; she hates me. My sisters don't listen when I talk; they are too busy putting me down. As far as my daddy goes, he could care less about my problems, so I am on my own. I hear people talking in church about how God bless them, and he can do the same for me. I cry because I just do not have the same experience as them. I have done everything to avoid temptation. It's like the more I don't give in to the devil, the more crap I go through. Why is my life so hard, Jesus? I can't understand. I walk out of the room in anger and sit on the stairs so Josh can't hear my frustration. I need a breakthrough, Jesus. Can I wake up one morning with happiness and peace and not worry about the pain I go through? "Mommy, I'm finished taking my bath."

"Okay, baby, get dressed, and don't forget to brush your teeth and say your prayers before going to bed."

He replied, "Yes, ma'am, I love you, Mommy."

I smile, "Love you too, baby," I walk downstairs into the kitchen, glancing at the clock on the wall. It is eight-forty-five p.m. already. I clean up the kitchen; I am sick of these roaches crawling over my sink. "Where did I do with that roach spray?" I looked underneath the kitchen sink and grabbed the spray; I began spraying everywhere. I hate this place. "Lord, why did you create roaches? What is their purpose here on earth? Are roaches a poor folks plague? Never mind, I just answered my question."

I cleaned the roaches and washed my hands to go upstairs to check on Josh. He's sleeping so peacefully; I've bent over and kissed him on the cheek. I stare at my son, mumbling; I wish I could do more for you, Josh. I am so sorry you have a failure as a mama. I walk out of his room and step into my room, flopping on the bed and crying. Why did you choose me, Lord? Why do I always have to struggle? Why do you keep blessing my sisters and cousins when you know they are living foul? It seems like I am never going to get up on my feet, Jesus. I do not want to go to church anymore. Maybe if I shack up with a man and playhouse like my sisters, and then perhaps you will bless me. They drive beautiful cars and travel, and their homes are not roach-infested like mines. I cried and cried until I cried myself to sleep.

Chapter 3

I woke up at six-thirty a.m.; I never sleep late. My body is a trained alarm clock. It automatically wakes up early. Thanks to my overprotective ex, Damon. He used to get up every morning for work back in the day before becoming a street hustler. Oh Lord, I wake up to a new day but the same situation once again. I wish food stamps would let you buy liquor. That is what I need this morning to help me get through this mess they call tribes and tribulations that are supposed to make us strong. I do not see how because I am falling apart by the minute. Today is Saturday, and I cannot even take my son anywhere special. I do not have the money to do anything. I leave my bed and walk downstairs to the kitchen and open my refrigerator. I   have only two slices of white bread left to feed my son. I look inside my cabinets, and It's bare. I thought you said you were supposed to supply all our needs, Lord? Well, I need food to feed my son. I slam the cabinets and sit at the dining room table. What am I going to do? I need more than $7.25 an hour to make it work. They cut my food stamps to $100. Lord, I do no t know how I'm going to make it. Josh comes downstairs and kisses me on the cheek, "Good morning, Mommy,"

"Good morning, sweetie. Why are you up so early,"

He smiles, "Mommy, can I watch cartoons in your room?"

"How about we give the cartoons a rest this morning? I want you to read the books Ms. Waters bought you for your birthday."

He pouts, "I want to watch cartoons.

"Do what I say. You will not watch cartoons for a week."

He gives me sad puppy eyes, "Yes, ma'am,"

I sigh as Josh walks upstairs. I don't feel like calling my mother. Please don't let her say anything to me to provoke me to go off on her. I need to say something so she can give me some money. Okay, here goes. I reach for my phone on the wall in the kitchen. A roach crawling on my wall as I dial my mother's number. I get a flyer from my kitchen drawer, smash the cockroach, and throw it in the garbage. My mother picks up on the four-ring. She answers the phone with a raspy voice, "Hello,"

"Hi, mama," my mama yawns into the phone, "Girl, do you know what time it is? Call me back."

I beg my mama, "Please don't hang up," my mama clears her throat before speaking, "What do you want, heifer?"

I breathe slowly through the phone before asking, "Can I borrow a couple of dollars mama?"

My mama's raspy voice went to a high pitch, "Borrow! You know goodness well. You can't pay me back."

I sigh, "Okay, mama, can I have some money?"

She said, "I don't have it right now."

"Well, do you at least have a dollar so I can get your grandson some Ramen noodles?"

My mama sucks her teeth, "You have no food?"

I replied with a sad tone, "No, ma'am,"

She asked, "What about your food stamps?"

Tears run down my face, "They cut me down $100 a month when I started back working."

My mom begins to fuss, "I just don't understand. You wasted six fucking years in college just to wind up working at some damn fast-food joint. I don't know why the hell you went to college because all that education didn't do a damn thing for you."

I scoff, "I had a good job before they laid me off, mama."

"The keyword is you had a job, all you have is some damn degree, what a waste. Look, get your ass dressed. I'll be over there in 30 minutes to pick you up. Lord knows I don't want my grandson to starve to death," I smile, wiping my tears away,

My mama replied, "You owe me; besides, I can't blame Josh for having a jacked-up ass mama with a stupid-ass master's degree that can't feed her child,"

I held my head down, "Mama, that's harsh." my mama replied, "Oh, shut up, you already know how I feel about you."

I cut my eyes toward the kitchen ceiling, "I know you regret having me, and you wish I were never born because your life could have been so much better. Yeah mama, I know the story." My mama hung up on me before I could say thank you. I guess that went well. I hang up the phone, run upstairs. I hope my mama gives me at least $50 worth of food. I walk into my room, and Josh is lying in bed reading his books. "Josh, go brush your teeth and wash your face; we are going to the store." Josh jumps out the bed with excitement, "Yes, ma'am,"

"When you get through in the bathroom, get your jeans and T-shirt at the draw."

He asked, "Mommy, can I wear my Spiderman shirt and black pants?"

I smiled, "Yes, and you can wear your black shoes." As soon as Josh came out of the bathroom, I went in to shower quickly and got dressed. Thank the Lord for my hair. I brush it back into a ponytail and let it air dry when it gets wet. I brush it back into a ponytail and let it air dry when it gets wet. I don't feel like putting on any earrings. I don't feel pretty at all; I feel like pure crap. Josh is sitting on the side of my bed, "Mommy, somebody is knocking at the door,"

I sigh, "That's probably your grandmother; I'll get it." I walked downstairs to open the door; it was my younger sister, Jada. I frowned.

"Hey," I block my front door entrance. Jada paused, looking confused, "Girl, move out of the way so I can come in."

I shake my head, "Oh no, I'm going to the store with my mama." Jada slightly pushes me out of the way, walking into my house. "Okay, I'll watch Josh while you go to the store." I closed the door and followed my sister to the bathroom as she was primping in the mirror, "Jada, no, my son is going with me. Now you need to leave."

Jada chuckles, "Girl, why are you tripping? I am not Damon," Josh walks downstairs. My sister comes out of the bathroom to greet him, "Hey baby,"

Josh frowned, "What happened to your hair, Auntie?"

She laughs, "You don't like it?"

He shakes his head, "No, ma'am, it looks like snakes in your hair." Jada rubs her hair, glaring at Josh. "Little man, you hurt Auntie's feelings. It's a straw set. I was trying something different with my hair. Do you like it, sis?"

I replied, "Not my style,"

"Forget y'all. I like it," she said.

"Well, if you like it, that's all that matters," she walks out the bathroom and flops down on the couch next to her nephew. I walk over to the window to keep an eye on my mama to pull up, "Jada, why are you at my house so early?"

She replied, "Girl, I went out with a couple of my girlfriends last night. We were drinking while having a good old time. My ass got drunk, and I had to sleep on my girl's couch last night." I glare at Jada, "So you decide to come over here; I'm so lucky."

She rubs her stomach, "What do you have to snack on?" I replied with a firm tone, "Nothing," she scanned my townhouse, "Girl, you need to get a better-paying job so you can get a nicer townhouse. I wouldn't be dead caught living like this."

I scoff, "Please, I don't feel like one of your lectures this morning,"

She smirked, "Fine, Josh, do you want to stay with auntie while your mama goes to the store?" he replied, "Yes, ma'am," I cut my eyes at Jada, "Fine, stay with your auntie," my house phone rang, I walk to the kitchen to answer the phone, "Hello,"

"I'm outside."

"I'm coming," I hang the phone up, "Okay, that's my mama, Josh. You behave, and you too, Jada,"

"Yeah, just go," said Jada as she closed the door behind me. I began walking to my mama's car. I glanced to my right and saw Gina sitting on the porch, drinking a beer early in the morning. She waves at me. I wave back and see Damon standing in the doorway, staring at me as I get into my mama's car, "Good morning, mama,"

She sighs heavily, "What is so good about it?" She glanced over to Gina, sitting on the porch drinking beer. "Why is Damon over at that girl's house early in the morning?"

I shrug my shoulders, "I don't know, mama,"

She said, "Hell, he should be giving your ass money; you didn't make Josh by yourself."

I sigh, "I know that mama." My mom blows the horn and signals Damon to come to the car. My mama rolls her window down as he approaches the vehicle, "Good morning, Ms. Howard,"

She said, "Let me ask you a question?"

"Yes, ma'am," my mama glanced at me, then back at Damon, "Why is my daughter calling me for money to buy food for my grandson?"

He replied, "Ms. Howard, I offered Shanel money yesterday and bought Burger Shop for Josh last night. She threw the food at me and said she did not want my money." My mama gave me a dirty look, "Why the hell did you do that, Shanel?"

I replied, "Mama, he was trying to give me blood money." My mama slapped me in the face. I grabbed my face, holding back my tears. Damon was caught by surprise, "Shit! What the hell? Ms. Howard, come on now, you didn't have to slap her." My mama glared at Damon and then turned to me. "Look, girl, nobody told you to open your legs to him. Now let me tell you all something; it's not about you or Damon; it's about my grandson. Blood money or not, you need money to take care of your son, Shanel."

I held my face fighting my tears back. "Mama, I'm not going to take his money,"

My mama shouts at me, "Yes, the hell you are. Damon is the man you chose to be with, so deal with it! Get your ass out of my car so Damon can take you to the store." I beg my mama, "Please, mama!"

My mama reached over me to open the passenger door and began shoving me out of her car. "Shanel, get your ass out my car now!"

I cried, "Okay!"

My mama yells, "Don't call me no more asking me for money when Damon is busting his ass in these streets to support y'all son."

I slam my mama's car door, "Don't be slamming my door, heifer!"

I shout with tears rolling down my face, "Just leave me alone, mama!"

She shouts out her car window, "You call me messing up my day with your stupid-ass foolishness." I moved out of the way as she backed out the parking lot, driving off without a care in the world. Damon looks at me, shaking his head, "What?" He walks toward me, looking at my face. "You need to put an ice pack on your face." I gave Damon that look, "Could you not look at me like that?"

"Go to hell, Damon."

He frowns, shaking his head, "Damn girl, can we just go to the store to get our son something to eat?" Gina comes walking toward us, "You okay, Damon?"

He looks in my direction when replying to Gina, "Yeah, I'm good. Go back inside the house?"

I frown, adding my two cents, "Yeah, go back inside the house and check on your man bitch." Damon was bewildered, "What the hell is wrong with you, Shanel? Gina has been my ace from day one. You need to check your fucking attitude."

I sigh, walking toward my townhouse and rubbing my bruised face. Damon follows behind me, calling my name, "Shanel," I turn around with tears in my eyes, answering in a harsh tone. "What, Damon?"

He said, "I'm waiting to take you to the store."

I asked, "For what?"

He clenched his jaws in anger, "Uh, we need to go get Josh some food, Shanel,"

I replied, "I'm not going with you, Damon."

"Damn, Shanel! Can you stop being so fucking selfish? Now it's obvious you don't have any money to buy food for our son. Now get your ass in the car so we can go buy our son some damn food!"

"I don't want your drug money, Damon."

Damon chuckles, "You so damn stupid. Where the hell do you think most of the money comes from, Shanel? It's all damn dirty, from drugs to prostitution, gambling, hell, the list goes on. You need to wake the fuck up, Shanel."

I lashed out angrily "I am tired of arguing with you about the same thing repeatedly, Damon. Sometimes I wish I never met your ass."

"Ditto," said Damon. Jada came outside looking confused, "What the hell is going on with you two?" I shove Jada out of the way, walking back to my townhouse.

"Your damn childish-ass sister," said Damon,

"Hey, do not be disrespecting my sister. Y'all need to come together and resolve your issues with each other," said Jada.

"Damon, come here now!" Said the old lady shouting across the street.

Jada points her finger toward the road, "Who is this old lady calling your name?" he turns toward the street, he sighs, "Ms. Waters," he walks toward the old lady, "Why the hell you out here fussing with Shanel?"

Damon frowns, "Because she is acting downright selfish, Ms. Water," she grabs Damon by the arm, "Walk with me over to the house."

"Can we talk after I come back from the store? I need to get my son food." She smiled, "Alright, just make sure you return back to my house when you finish."

"Yes, ma'am," he walks toward Jada, "What did she want?" Damon shunned Jada and began walking to his car.

Jada asked, "Damon, will you talk to my sister?"

He replied, "No, I'm going to the store to buy my son some food." Damon got into his car, and I stood on my porch, watching him drive off. My sister Jada joins me on the porch, "What is going on with you and Damon? And what happened to your face? Did he hit you?"

I snap at Jada, "No, just leave it alone; it doesn't concern you."

"Yes, it does; you are my sister, Shanel."

I replied, "Trust me to let it go, Jada. I will be fine,"

Jada glares at me, "Yeah, right, so why were y'all yelling at each other, acting like backwoods niggers just a minute ago?"

I softly replied, "I'm not in the right state of mind for your questions about my life." Jada sighs as I walk back into my townhouse and lock myself in the bathroom, crying. Jada walked in and closed the door calling my name. "Shanel, where are you?"

Josh walks halfway downstairs, "Auntie Jade, what's wrong with my mommy?" Jade walks to the steps, "Your mom is a little upset right now, go upstairs to your room and watch cartoons."

Josh frowned, "Yes, ma'am, Auntie Jada. Can I have butterscotch candy, please?"

Jada walks to the couch to get the candy out of her purse, "Here you go, baby, now go back upstairs in the room and watch TV."

Jada walks to the bathroom door, "Shanel, come out of the bathroom,"

I replied, "No, Jada!" Jada bangs on the bathroom door, "Shanel, come out of that bathroom right now before I break this door down!"

I scream, "Leave me the hell alone!" Jada walks away from the bathroom door and grabs her cell phone from her purse, "I'm going to call Sharon if you don't get out that bathroom!" Jada calls Sharon. She answers on the second ring, "Hey Jada, what's up?"

"You need to come over to Shanel's house,"

"Why?" asked Sharon.

"Shanel and Damon got into another argument again,"

Sharon sucks her teeth, "Jada, I am not going over there again. Her ungrateful ass kicked me out of her townhouse yesterday. See if I give her any more of my designer clothes. Beside my man is over here today, and he needs all my attention. Shanel is a grown woman. Tell her to pray or read the Bible or something."

Jada frowns, "you a cold woman,"

She laughs, "Just like those cold showers you take every night. Get a man, Jada."

"Girl, bye," Jada got off the phone as I came out of the bathroom. I walked toward my living room window, opened the curtains, and sat down on my comfort zone chair. I watched people interact outside. Jada sits on the couch, "Are you okay, Shanel,"

I sigh heavily, "Yeah."

"Are you sure?"

I answer in a firm voice, "Yes, Jada, now do me a favor and leave my townhouse,"

Jada replied, "I am not leaving; we need to talk about you. Why are you treating Damon like shit on toilet paper? That man is fine as wine. He is trying to do right with his son. Shit, if you do not want his fine ass, I'll be glad to take him off your hands."

I chuckled, shaking my head, "I will slap the hell out of your ass. You can't understand how I feel. I don't hate him."

Jada is confused, "Then what is it?"

I sigh, looking out the window, frowning. "Speaking of the devil, he's walking to my door." Jada gets up from the couch and opens the door for Damon, "Thanks, Jada. Where is Shanel?" asked Damon,

Jada points toward the couch, "Sitting in front of the window," Damon slams the grocery on the table, "Uh, can you help out with the groceries?"

I replied, "I can, but I prefer to sit by the window, minding my business."

Damon mumbles under his breath, "Whatever, Shanel,"

"I'll help you," said Jada. They both went out the front door. My phone rang, and I got up to answer it. Damon walks back into the house while I am on the phone. "Hello,"

"Hey, Shanel,"

"Hey, Doug, can I call you back later?"

Damon slams the bags on the table, "This is the last bit of groceries," Jada comes in with two bags of chips, smiling, "Thanks, Damon, this should last for a while," She sat the bags on the table.

Damon glances at Shanel, "Can you please let my son know he has food to eat."

I sigh, "Yes, and Damon,"

"What?"

I calmly said, "Thanks," Damon was caught off guard by my gesture, "All right, I'm out."

Jada walks him out the front door, "Uh, Shanel, I will be right back. Uh, Damon, can I talk to you for a minute?"

He sighs, looking annoyed, "Sure, what you want to talk about, Jada?"

She whispers, "Let's walk away from the door so Shanel won't hear us," His cell phone vibrates in his jean pocket. He pulls his cell phone out to answer, "Hold up, I need to take this call. What's good, D-Man?"

"I need you to come to Cali as my studio engineer." Damon smiled, looking toward Shanel's townhouse, "Aiight, D-Man, I'm down. When do you need me?" He said, "Right now, muthafucka, let's get this paper,"

Damon laughs, "Aiight; I'll make it happen."

Damon hangs up his cell with a huge smile on his face.

Jada asked, "Good news,"

Damon smiles, "Yeah,"

Jada and Damon walk toward his car, "Now, back to you and my sister. What happened between you and Shanel? You all were so happy together."

Damon replied, leaning against his car with his arms folded up. "Her fucking mama interfered, turning her head against me. You know how Ms. Howard can be. I did not come from a well-to-do family. I am from Compton, Ca, and that pissed Shanel's mama the hell off. My mama did the best she could to raise my knucklehead brothers and me to keep us off the streets. So, we moved to Atlanta when I was fifteen for a so-called better life. No matter what my hustle may be, I am a good man taking care of my son."

"Then prove it. I know you still care about my sister." Said Jada

Damon cleared his throat, "How the hell you figure that?"

Jada smiled, "Do you want me to answer that?"

 He chuckles, "Yeah, I do,"

Jade smiles, shaking her head, "Okay, Damon, why are you always over at Gina's house all the damn time?"

He unfolds his arms, laughing. "We play spades,"

Jada gives him a rising eyebrow, "Y'all play spades every day, c'mon Damon, you talking to me, Jada."

Damon continues laughing at Jada, "Yes, we do. Besides, Gina is my homegirl; we go way back to high school."

Jada smiles, "How convenient that Gina stays next door to the mother of your child."

Damon shuns Jada, "You just make sure your sister feeds my son. I got to go."

Jada smirks, "Alright, Damon, but I know you still love my sister,"

Damon gets into his car, smiling at Jada, "Nice car, how can you afford a custom-made BMW, Damon?"

Damon cranks up his car, "Bye, Jada," he drives across the street to see that old lady. Jada walks back to her sister's townhouse.

Chapter 4

Jada walks into the house after talking to Damon. She frowns, "Damn, Shanel, you could at least put up the food and stop staring at the window,"

I replied, "I could have, but I didn't,"

Jada walks toward me, "You need to swallow your pride, Shanel, and appreciate what Damon is doing for his son,"

I continue looking out the window, "Jada, please, you don't know shit,"

She said, "You're right, but what I do know is that Damon is a great dad trying his best to do right by his son."

I sigh, "With drug money, Jada,"

Jada sat on the couch across from me, "Girl, stop tripping. Money is money. You shouldn't give a damn where it comes from. As long as he can care for Josh and your household, you should be grateful."

I chuckle, "You would say some crap like that,"

Jada smirks, "I say it with no shame either," Jada gets up from the comfort zone couch, putting up the food. She calls for Josh to come downstairs. He quickly comes downstairs, "Yes, ma'am," Jada asked, "Do you want a pizza?"

Josh follows his auntie into the kitchen, "Yes, ma'am, may I have a cheese pizza?"

Jada smiled, "Cheese pizza it is, little man. Now go back upstairs, and I'll call you when the pizza is ready."

Josh walks into the living room, "Mama, I love you,"

I smile and motion for him to hug me, "I love you too,"

Josh walks back upstairs to watch cartoons in my room. Jada smiles at me as she is getting a plate out the cabinet, "Ahh shit! How do you deal with these fucking roaches, Shanel?"

I calmly replied, "I don't,"

Jada asked, "Where is your spray?"

I said, "It's underneath the kitchen sink,"

Jada got the can of roach spray and began spraying it all over my cabinet, "Damn girl, it's too many roaches. I can't live like this, and neither should you." She threw the empty roach spray in the trash. Jada washed her hands along with Josh's plate for his pizza. She asked, "How you work your microwave, Shanel?"

I said, "Just push pizza."

Jada walks toward me and sits beside me on the couch. "Shanel, what are you going to do?"

I gave Jada a puzzled look, "What are you talking about?"

Jade replied, "Duh, about your situation, you are a smart woman with a master's degree, and you are living like a poor person,"

I turned toward my sister, "I am so sick and tired of you lecturing me. I have sent my resume out to banks and marketing firms. You name it. I sent it out. I can't make nobody give me a damn job,"

"I understand, Shanel, but you do not give up either. Keep sending your resumes out until somebody calls you," said Jada.

I got irritated with Jada, "Who said I am giving up? I am not giving up. I wish you, Sharon, and Cousin Melissa would stay out of my business. Nobody said shit to you three when you all were having a hard time finding jobs. I would appreciate it if you all would give me the same damn respect."

Jada frowned, "Why do you get so angry when people are trying to give you advice?"

I angrily replied, "I get angry because you are always putting me down. I did not put myself in this situation. My firm fired everybody in my department. You know what, get out of my damn house. I am getting tired of having to keep explaining my situation to you and the rest of the damn family."

Jada gets up from the couch, "Fine! If you want to live with roaches in this nasty ass townhouse, then go right ahead."

"Shut up, Jada; I don't have a mama like you to rescue me every time I have a problem."

Jada momentarily froze in her tracks. She could not move. I gave her a crazy-ass look, "Jada, what's wrong with you?"

She snaps back, putting on her heels, "What about Daddy?"

I sigh, "The donor! He never helped me, hell I do not recall the donor showing up to any of my track meets."

Jada has a confused look on her face, "Shanel, Daddy has always been there for his children,"

I harshly said, "You a damn lie. The donor you call daddy did not come to my graduation, Jada."

Jada frowns, "Yes, he did, Shanel,"

I stared Jada down, "No, he did not. Go upstairs and look inside my nightstand on the right-hand side of my bed. You will see all the letters I wrote to the donor you call Daddy. You will get a kick out of his response."

Jada walks upstairs into my bedroom; I hear her opening my nightstand drawer. I walk into the kitchen to see what Damon bought for his son to eat. Damn, he went all out, I can't complain, but he just makes me mad, God. I know Damon is smart; I just hate that he took the fast way of life to make a living. I walk back to my comfort zone couch as Jada comes downstairs with all my rejection letters in her hand from the donor, they call daddy. She laid them on my scratched-up wooden coffee table.

Jada said, "I'll be right back; I need to take my nephew his pizza and drink."

I glanced at the letters with anger, shaking my head. Jada closed my room door and walked back downstairs, "Okay, I see all the letters," said Jada. She sat in the chair across from me, she began reading the envelopes, "Why do they say return to sender?" I gave Jada the side eye. "The donor you call daddy returned every letter I wrote to him except for the graduation invitation. He sent me a fuck you letter. Maybe you should read that one to get an idea of how the donor you call daddy feels about his firstborn." Jada sighed, rolling her eyes at me as she took out the letter from the envelope. Jada begins reading the letter. "No dear or nothing,"

"To the daughter, I did not want; I wish you would stop wasting your time writing to me. Common sense would tell you if I haven't come to any of your school activities, what makes you think I'm going to break my neck to come to your high school graduation? I had told your mother when you were born, I didn't want to be a part of your life. I wanted my firstborn to be a son; it disappointed me when I saw you in the hospital baby nursery dressed in pink. You and your mother have cursed my life. All my siblings' firstborns were boys. I will never forgive your manipulating mother for not aborting you. Your mother is a whore. I would appreciate it if you would stop sending me pictures of you and your son. I only have two daughters, Sharon and Jada. I will always be there for them and love them dearly. One more thing, every time Sharon calls me, she has nothing nice to say about you. Jada doesn't even mention you at all. I believe in my heart that Sharon and Jada are only nice because you are their blood sister. I told them that you are a disgrace to my family and that you would never amount to anything in life. They should not have to be nice to trash. Your sisters have nice jobs, doing well for themselves. Unlike you, who has a child out of wedlock and lives in a rundown community with a minimum wage job driving a junkyard car. You are worthless, just like your mother, and this is my first and last letter to you. If you send me any more letters, I will have them returned. Good riddance." Jada holds her chest in disbelief with tears rolling down her face, "Shanel, I'm so sorry,"

I chuckled, "No, you're not,"

Jada wiped her tears away, "How are you going to tell me how I feel?"

I replied, "Because you did not have any sympathy for me until you read what the donor you call daddy wrote to me. You swore up and down that the donor you call daddy was there for me."

Jada flips through my rejection letters, "I just assume…"

"Exactly, you are always assuming, and I just feel like I have been fucking exiled out of my own family. I don't have family reaching out to me. My mother was never there for me; I had to learn how to take care of myself. She didn't teach me anything about the birds and the bees. Are how to take care of myself when I began my menstrual. When I first came on my menstrual in sixth grade, I thought my ass was dying. All the boys were picking on me because I had a big red stain on my dress. My teacher took me to the bathroom, helping me clean myself up. She sent me to the school nurse to get sanitary napkins. The school nurse had to tell me that my body was going through changes. If it was not for my teacher and the school nurse, I would have still been walking around in bloody panties every month." Jada held her head down in shame, "Shanel…I don't know what to say, but trust God,"

I sigh sharply, "Oh, please! He does not answer my prayers; I think he had it in for me when I was born. I go to church, and the preacher always closes his sermon with this passage, For God so loved the world, that he gave his only begotten Son." Jada wipes her tears away, "God does love you, Shanel." I get up from my comfort zone couch, walk toward the window, looking up to the heavens. "Yeah, right, Jada, then why did the donor you call daddy reject me because I wasn't a boy? Why does my mama treat me like I'm not her daughter?" Jada sighed, wiping her tears as I continued talking with pain pouring out of my heart, "Let's talk about you, Sharon, and Cousin Melissa. You guys are just as worst as the donor you call daddy." I walked into the kitchen to get a bottle of water that Damon bought earlier today. Jada follows behind me. "I just want to see you get out of your situation Shanel." I sipped my water, as Jada sat on my countertop. "Watch out for the roach Jada," she jumped down quickly. I walk upstairs to check on my son, "You okay, Josh?"

He smiles, "Yes, ma'am, I am full from eating my pizza," I take his plate and cup downstairs. Jada is sitting on my comfort zone couch, going through her cell phone. I wash out Josh's cup and plate and join my sister on the comfort zone couch, looking out the window. I shake my head watching this lady buying drugs from a teenager. I sigh looking at Jada going through her phone. "So, six months ago, I began reading Job's story in the Bible, and did you know God allowed the devil to try his servant, Job?"

Jada paused from her cell phone, "I know you are not comparing yourself to Job? He was rich before and after his tribe and tribulations,"

"I may not have been rich, Jada, but I had a great job, lived in a gorgeous townhome, and paid my titles every time I got paid. I don't understand why God allowed the devil to bring me down?"

"Shanel, you shouldn't be mad at God; he's only trying to correct the ones he loves."

"I replied angrily, "He should be correcting you, Sharon, the donor you call daddy, my mother, and Damon's ass. Goodness gracious, I was celibate for seven years before I had my son. I don't go to nightclubs or sleep with different men every day of the week."

Jada became annoyed, "Okay, I get it, Shanel, we bad, and you, Ms. Perfect,"

I lash out, "Ugh! You don't get it, Jada,"

Jada said, "Look, Shanel; I'm sorry Daddy disowned you but don't punish your sisters for his wrongdoing,"

I begin to cry, "You and Sharon are spoiled. Your mothers and the donor you call daddy put band-aids on every situation that came up against you all. You and Sharon will never know how it is to struggle truly."

Jada walks into the bathroom to get me some tissue to wipe my face, "You're right, Shanel; I am thankful for my mama and our daddy that they didn't let me struggle. Shanel, you are the strongest sibling, whether you like it or not." Tears flooded my face, "I just want to pass the cup to you and Sharon. I am tired of my life." Jada frowns, "You can keep your cup, just like Jesus had to keep his cup to full his purpose on this earth." Jada went back to looking through her cell phone, "Jada, let me ask you a question?"

She said, "Ask away my sister,"

"Okay, why do you keep coming over to my townhouse? Huh?" She paused from her cell phone, looking confused. "Duh, because you are my sister," I got irritated, with her calm response, "So why don't you and Sharon invite me over to y'all apartment?"

Jada glanced at me with a little smirk, "Huh?"

"You heard me, and I don't have any of y'all addresses. Why is that, Jada?" she put her phone down on the coffee table, "Because…"

Jada bites the bottom of her lip as she did when she was a little girl, "I'm waiting for an answer, Jada,"

She sighs, "I don't know, Shanel,"

"Yes, you do. You, Sharon, and Melissa like to use me. I used to do your hair, and all of you heifers didn't even pay me, but you and Sharon will pay your beautician a hundred dollars to do the same damn thing I did for free. That's why I stop doing your hair. You know what, get the hell out of my damn house, and don't bring your ass back."

Jada was shocked, "You don't mean that, Shanel,"

I get up from my comfort zone couch walking to the door, "Yes, I do, and you can pass the message on to Sharon and Melissa," I open my front door,

"Fine! You know what? Daddy was right about you. You are a sorry-ass bitch who is not going to amount to shit! You will keep on struggling for the rest of your natural bone life. I will call Sharon and Melissa on you so they can talk some sense into your thick head." Jada grabs her purse leaving my townhouse. I laughed when she almost tripped walking to her Lexus that the donor, they call daddy bought as a gift for graduating from college. I slammed the door, locking it behind me so she wouldn't try to come back into my townhouse. I check on Josh; he has fallen asleep watching cartoons. As soon as I get myself together, I am leaving Norcross, Ga, for good. I reached for my Bible off my dresser, closed my room door, and went back downstairs to sit on my comfort zone couch to read my Bible. As I begin reading, my phone rings. I get up to answer the phone, "Hello,"

"Shanel, this is Ms. Waters, I am going to send Damon over to you, so you all can have a decent conversation. It doesn't make sense for you all to be fussing and caring on; you two have a son. So, I'm going to ask you all to handle that shit. You all done fucked up my nerves. I'm going to have to smoke a bat tonight." I sigh, "Ms. Waters, I was about to read my Bible; I'm not in the move to talk to Damon right now." Her voice turns firm, "You need to make the damn time; he's on his way to your house." She hangs up the phone; I walk to my comfort zone couch, punching the hell out my frumpy pillows until I was interrupted by a knock at my front door. I sigh, putting the pillow back on the comfort zone couch, then look at the window before opening the door for Damon. I ask him in a calm voice, "What do you want?" he looks me in the eye, "May I come in and have a decent conversation with the mother of my son?" I nod. He walked in and sat down right in my seat, moving my Bible to the coffee table, "you are reading the Bible?"

I rub my temples, sitting on the arm of my sofa across for Damon. "I was. Now what do you want to talk about?"

He said, "Real talk, what the hell happened to us, Shanel?" He caught me by surprise with that question. I could not answer, "Damon, why are you worried about us now? We have been over for a year now."

He said, "I know that. Let me ask you a question. Do you hate my black ass? Because we cannot have a decent conversation without fussing, that shit needs to stop." I sigh, tapping the side of my thigh. "Damon, I do not hate you. I just wish you made better decisions for yourself. You are a brilliant man with so much talent. I smile. Do you remember when I was pregnant with our son? You used to write many rap songs and be in the studio doing your thang. What happened to that drive you used to have, Damon?" He looks at me, getting up from the sofa and pulling me toward him. We flopped down on the comfort zone couch together. "You and Josh were my inspiration, then after we broke up, I was like fuck it, I don't give a damn no more."

I shake my head, "So you are blaming me?"

He rubs his head, "No, I blame myself for not continuing my dreams; I shouldn't let my fucking anger get the best of me."

"I used to tell you that when we were dating. I said, you needed to stop being so quick to get angry over the petty mess that your cousin used to do all the time. He sighs, "I need to get my ass right before I am in somebody's cemetery. Just like you need to stop being so comfortable sitting on the couch that you call your comfort zone." I shake my head, "Please don't, I'm not in the move." Damon rubs his hands together, looking at me, "I'm just saying we both have to make some changes regarding our son. You just need to chill and stop fussing with your damn family and me. The more you stress, the less you focus on your goals."

I smile, "That's something Ms. Water would say."

We both laugh, "You aren't slick; how are you going to bite off her words of wisdom?"

He smiles, "I'm just happy we are laughing and not fussing."

I sigh, "Yeah, we used to have some good time…" he interrupts me, "We are having a moment. Don't spoil it with the past." We both went silent. Damon broke the ice. He said, "So I won't be around for a while. I have some projects I am working on." I glance at Damon, "Where are you going?"

He said, "I don't wanna say just yet,"

I frown, "why not?"

"Shanel, just trust me for once in your life." I replied in a calm tone, "Okay, fine, Damon,"

He gets up from the sofa, "Look, I'm going to get out here. You take care of my son." He let himself out, locking the door behind him. Lord, I hope he gets it together for his son. I'm tired. I reach for my Bible, reading the 121 Psalms.

Chapter 5

It has been two weeks since I have spoken to Jada, Sharon, or Damon. It has been peaceful, even when I go to work at my minimum-wage job. I have a smile on my face, my manager Doug gave me extra hours last week, and this week I am so happy. Oh shit! I spoke too damn soon. Gina comes walking her ass on my job with those tight jeans knowing goodness well it doesn't do anything for her big muffin top. "Shanel, have you heard from Damon?"

I roll my eyes, "I'm not his personal assistant Gina,"

She said, "Calm down, we haven't seen him in almost two weeks I'm just concerned,"

I frown, "Then, you should call him instead of coming to my job." Gina shakes her head, "Let me get a number one with the works and coke. Shanel, you may be bitter toward Damon, but he loves his son,"

I sigh, "For your information, I'm not bitter, just tired of Damon dropping in and out whenever he feels like it. I am not going to stress over his inconsistent ass. That will be six dollars and fifty-two cents."

Gina gave me the exact change, "Here is your receipt,"

I fixed Gina's drink and her meal since we are short staff tonight. I place her order on the counter, "Have a good night,"

Gina cuts her eyes at me, "Whatever, Shanel, you need to grow the hell up and let Damon be the dad he wants to be for his son. He loves Josh."

I stared her down, "Gina, you are concerned about the wrong damn thing. Please stay in your lane. Next customer, please." Gina grabs her food and turns to the guy behind her hugging him, "What's up, Greg? I haven't seen you in a while."

He smiles, "I know, right; I had to leave the fast life alone and settle down."

Gina is shocked, "What? I didn't know you got married." I continued listening to the conversation and taking customer orders while Gina was flirting and running her damn mouth.

He asked Gina, "How is my boy, Damon doing?"

She glances in my direction, "I don't know, ask his difficult baby mama."

He turns to me, smiling. I frown; he turns back to Gina. "She seems angry." They both chuckle, and Gina hugs him. "Alright, I'll let my husband know I bumped into you today. You and the wifey are more than welcome to the house to play spade with the hubby and me."

He said, "I will take you up on that offer if my wife says it's okay."

Gina laughs, "oh, you in ball and chain marriage."

He laughs, "None of that,"

Gina said, "Alright, take it easy, Greg." Then she looks in my direction, shaking her head, walking out of my job. She has some nerve; she needs to worry about her own life instead of mine. I glance at the clock on the wall; ten minutes' left before quitting time. "Shanel, I need to talk to you when you get through with that customer.

"Okay, Doug," the customer smiled, "You Damon woman?" my smile fades away quickly, "Wrong, I'm the mother of his son."

"My bad, I overheard Gina mention Damon's name; he's, my homeboy. We used to hang back in the day before I got married."

I smirk, "Good for you. May I take your order now?"

He chuckles, "May I have a number three, please?"

I fix his drink, "Here you go." He puts his straw in his cup, looking at me, "Can you tell Damon that Greg said Hey?" I glare at him, "That will be six dollars and seventy-five cents." Doug sat his order next to my register. I hand him his meal, "Have a great night." He grabs his bag, "I guess Damon hasn't given up the hood, huh?"

I asked him, "Why would you say that?"

He sips his drink before answering, "The conversation you had with Gina was kinda cold. I know what kind of company Gina and her man keep around them."

I said, "Greg, this conversation is over, have a good night."

He chuckles, "You need to cut that man some slack. He has a lot of things on his plate right now."

I get spicy with Greg, "And so do I. What's your point?"

He scoffs, "He doesn't need to deal with an angry baby mama. He needs your support."

I quickly set him straight, "I am not angry. Hold up…why am I explaining myself to you? You don't even know me, so back the hell out of my business." Greg sighs, walking away, mumbling to himself, "What the hell did Damon get himself into, that bitch got some serious issue." I took the last customer order then I walked to the grill to see why Doug wanted to talk to me. "What's up, Doug?

He asked, "Are you okay?

I replied, "I'm good. That was one of Damon's boys from back in the day dipping in the business that doesn't concern him."

Doug is flipping the burgers, "Okay, Shanel, I'm sorry to do this to you, but I need you to stay till closing; Lamar called out again. That man is on thin ice with me,"

I said, "Sure, I just need to call Ms. Waters and let her know."

Doug smiled, "Do what you have to do and then get on that grill Shanel," I walked to the office to call Ms. Waters to let her know that I would be late tonight. She answers on the third ring coughing on the phone, "Hello."

"Hey, Ms. Waters, this Shanel," she clears her throat, "I know who this is. What you want, sweetie?"

I sigh, "We short staff, so I have to stay late."

She coughs, trying to talk and clear her throat, "You make that money, Josh is sleeping, and I have a visitor, so you can pick him up in the morning."

I chuckle, "Okay, thanks," I hang up with Ms. Waters and walk into the freezer to grab more hamburgers patties to put on the grill, "Doug, why didn't Carlos clean the damn grill before he left?"

"Shanel, I don't have time to babysit grown-ass men, just clean the grill and cook the burgers, please." I frown while cleaning the grill, "Doug, you need to do a better job hiring employees that want to work." Doug chuckles, "Shanel, I hear you now drop twenty burgers. We have a basketball team walking through the door."

I get irritated, "What the hell, Doug? I haven't finished cleaning the grill,"

Doug shouted, "fuck the grill, drop the burgers, and make sure they are seasoned,"

I suck my teeth, "Okay, Doug, I'll do what I can," I begin dropping the burgers on the grill, seasoning, and searing each burger. I shouted, "fifteen minutes on the burgers, Doug," Damn, this grill is hot. I'm sweating, I walk to the soda fountain to get myself something to drink. I hear the boy's college basketball team talking about the ass-whipping they gave on the court tonight that led to their victorious win. I chuckled. Doug shouts, "Shanel, how much longer on the burgers?" I rush back to the grill, "Uh, eleven minutes Doug,"

He yells out in frustration, "Somebody, please call Lamar's ass and tell him he's fucking fired!" I laugh at Doug. He always says that every time somebody calls out, we get slammed.

He walks back to the grill, "How much longer on the burgers, Shanel?"

"Nine minutes to go, Doug,"

"Shit! Drop twenty more as soon as they come off," said Doug. He walks back to the front end to keep an eye on things. I drink my soda patiently, waiting for the timer on the burgers to go off. Doug walks toward the grill frowning. "Damn, we got seven minutes to go. Shit, I am so fucking tempted to put the burgers in the microwave." I laugh, "You need to chill the hell out and give the guys free apple pies."

He smiles, "Good looking out, Shanel." He walks back to the front passing out apple pies. Dana shouted, "Shanel, you got a phone call." Before I could respond, Doug told Dana to take a message. "Damn, Doug."

He said, "Sorry, Shanel, we busy right now," the timer goes off, and I shouted, "Burgers up," Doug and Samuel helped me get the burgers off the grill. Doug gets agitated with the cashiers, "Hey ladies, you all stop flirting and start making these guy burgers, stay focused! Come on, team, we are almost finished! Shanel, drop twenty more burgers." I wipe the sweat from my head with a damp cloth, "Okay, Doug, I'm on it." I walk back to the freezer to get more burgers. Doug calls me to the front, "Doug, can I drop the burgers first, gees?" After I drop the burgers, I walk to the front. Somebody is here to see you. I glance over Doug's shoulder, "Can I help you?" the young man smiles, "My name is Darryl," I give him a confused look, "Do I know you?" he sighs, fidgeting with his hands, his lips trembling, "Yes…No I'm…we our…never mind, this was a mistake." He rushed out The Burger Shop without ordering anything, and it was one o'clock in the morning. I don't have time to entertain dumb ass people. I walk back to the grill seasoning the burgers.

Doug walks toward me, "Who was that strange guy asking for you?"

I replied in a calm tone, "I don't know, and I don't care,"

"Well, I hope he's not stalking you?" said Doug,

I frown with concern, "Stalking me; you think he is trying to kill me?"

Doug stares at me, "I don't know, Shanel; just be careful. There's a lot of crazy people in the world."

My heart begins beating fast, "Now you got my ass paranoid. How the hell did he know my name?" Shit, I may need to get a gun to protect my son and me."

Doug shakes his head, "Just let Damon know what's going on."

I start thinking to myself, "Hold up, let's slow it down. It could be nothing. You got me all to wind up over nothing. He could be a friend of Gina or my sister's. Who knows,"

Doug said, "Okay if you say so, Shanel. Hey, since the crowd has died down, you can leave. Samuel and I can handle the cleaning. Thanks for staying late."

I smile, "You welcome, Doug, don't forget the burgers on the grill." I walk to the back to grab my belongings and clock out. Dana pined the message on the board. I frown when I see Damon's name. Dana shouted, "Shanel, did you get the message to call Damon?"

"Yes, thanks. Good night people," I walk out to my car, thank goodness Ms. Waters let Josh spend the night. She's like a grandmother to him. She never had any children, and that is why she spoils Josh. I love her like a mother. Ms. Waters always tells me to hold my head up and praise the Lord for the good and the bad. Ms. Waters always says to me to watch God move in my life for the good. I do not agree with Ms. Waters about Damon going to change and ask for my hand in marriage. I rebuke that in the name of Jesus. I get in my car, trying to crank it up; It's going to take me at least five minutes to get this car started, which I don't look forward to."

"Hey, Shanel," I turn to my right, "Hey, Danielle," she is smoking a cigarette, which I can't stand. She asked, "Are you having car trouble?"

I frown, "Always,"

She smiles, "At least it gets you where you need to go."

"Yeah," she finally put her cancer stick out, "What time does Dana get off from work."

I replied, "I think two a.m.,"

Danielle complains, "Girl, I'm tired of getting out of bed at one-thirty to pick my sister up from work. I will be glad when she gets her car." I begin cranking up my car again and shout, "It started! Thank you, Jesus," Danielle smiled, "All right, Danielle, let me get out of here before my car cuts off on me."

She waves, "Bye, Shanel," I hate driving home alone. My mind begins to wander to my struggles. I just don't understand why I had to be born into an evil family. Why did I have to become a failure in the family? That is something I will never know the answers to that riddle. The red light caught me, and I prayed my car does not cut off on me. I look around for the police; I pause. Is that the donor they call daddy car? Nah, he wouldn't be out this time in the morning in my neck of the woods. The light finally turns green; I drive off with a massive cloud of smoke following behind me. I need to make it home before my car cuts off on me. I have one more block to go before I make it back to the townhouse. I'm glad nobody is driving behind me because they wouldn't be able to see anything. Damn, I hate this car. I finally pulled up to my townhouse, cutting off my vehicle. It shakes three times before it completely turns off. I grab my belongings and begin walking to the front door.

My ass froze in my tracks when I see Damon sitting in front of my door, "What are you doing here? It's almost two in the morning." he sighs, "Can we talk Shanel without all the arguing?" I look up at the midnight sky, then back at Damon, "Where is your car?" He looks around, "I parked it on the other side of the complex so Gina and her man wouldn't see me," I shake my head, "You know she came to my job looking for you, and some dude named Greg told me to tell you Hey." Damon chuckles, "That's my boy; we used to hang out every day until he found him a good-ass broad." I cut my eyes at him, "Why she got to be a broad?" he sighs, "My bad, young lady." I open my door, "Come in but don't turn the lights on yet. I set my bag on the table, feeling my way to the kitchen to get the roach spray I left on the counter, "Now turn on the lights, Damon,"

"Oh shit! Roach everywhere." Damon went back outside; I began spraying everywhere. I saturated the floor, so the roaches crawling on the ceiling would fall to the floor. I threw the empty can of roach spray in the garbage and washed my hands at the bathroom. "Okay, it's safe to come back in now. Just watch where you walk."

Damon peaked in, "You sure about that?"

I said, "Then stay outside," I walked upstairs to my bedroom, and Damon came in and closed the door behind him, "I'm going to have to move you out of this roach motel for real," he followed me upstairs. I cut my eyes at Damon as I took my shoes off and lay across my bed. Damon joins me in bed. "What do you want, Damon?"

He asked, "Where is my son?"

I yawned, "He's with Ms. Waters," He smiled, "So you by yourself?"

I frown, rubbing the side of my face, "Yes, Damon, now speak,"

"We need to talk about us, Shanel?"

I asked, "Uh, didn't we have this conversation two weeks ago?"

"Yes, we did, Shanel. I'm talking about being good parents to Josh without all the arguing. It's not healthy for him,"

"So, what will you do to change, Damon?"

"I been thinking a lot, and it was hard for me to tell you…"

I get up from the bed and turn to Damon, cutting him off, "Tell me what, Damon?" He takes a deep breath, "I'm moving back to

California to work with my Ace, he has a recording studio, and he wants me to help him run it."

I calmly asked, trying to fight back my damn tears, "Is that so? So, you were in California for two weeks? Was this the project you were talking about?"

He smiles, "Yeah, Shanel, it's a great opportunity for me," I get up from the bed walking to the bathroom. He grabs me by the arm, "Shanel, are you crying?"

"What about your son?" Damon pulled me into him gently. I sat on his lap with my head on his chest as he wiped my tears away, "Shanel, I will not leave you here by yourself to take care of my responsibility. I want to move you out of this hellhole tomorrow." "How Damon, you don't have any money," I slide off his lap on to the bed, "Shanel, you don't know what I have. I have been in California for the last two weeks making honest money. Hell, I make more money working in the recording studio than I did on the streets."

I fidget with my hair, "Okay, Damon, where are you moving us to?" he smiles as he massages my legs, "Sugarloaf in a gated community. I already bought the townhome." I get excited, jump onto my bed, and begin jumping up and down like a little kid. "Are you serious?"

He laughs, "Yes, Shanel, and please don't tell your family. Can you please stop jumping in the bed?"

"Yes, and trust me, Damon, my mouth is on lockdown. Since you are in the massaging mood, can you give me a neck massage?"

He said, "Yeah, lay across the bed," he sat beside me, working his magic relieving the stress out my body, girl you are so tense," he continued, massaging my neck and back, "Damon, what made you change your mind?" he sighs, "My boy, he changed my mind mentally about my life."

I asked, "So why are you helping me?"

He sighs, "Shanel, why do you have to ask so many damn fucking questions?"

I said, "Because I don't like to be freakin blindsided in situations, so I ask questions,"

He kissed the back of my neck, "Well, to answer your question, I'm tired of the mother of my son suffering and your family taking advantage of you. Especially your mother. She gave you hell the entire time we were dating."

I sigh heavily, "Don't remind me," Damon continues talking and massaging my neck, "I couldn't understand how your mother would make you work and just take your entire check. She would go clubbing with different men, buy clothes, and keep her hair and nails laced every week."

I get up from the bed, "Thanks for the massage. You know my mother is a selfish bitch. I wonder every day, why she even had me because my mama and daddy disowned me. I'm alone." Damon yawns before speaking, "No, you are not. You have Josh and me, don't worry about your sisters and cousin Melissa either."

"Easy said than done, Damon,"

He sighs, "Girl leaves them where they are, all right? Now, this is the plan for today, I want you to leave all this furniture in this townhouse. I do not want any roaches following you over to your new townhome. I'll hire somebody to move this crap. My cousin will pick you up this afternoon. Gina and her husband should be at church around that time." The corners of my mouth turned up, "Okay, I'm down with the plan."

I walk into the bathroom to turn the shower on, then step back into the room, looking at Damon laying across my bed. "Can you stay for a while?"

He grins from ear to ear, "Yeah, I can do that."

"Thanks," I grab my clothes out of the drawer, walking to the bathroom, locking the door behind me. I quickly got undressed, getting into the shower. I embrace the warm downpour caressing my tired body. As I lather my washcloth, slowly washing my body, I thank God for touching Damon's heart to do right by his son. I quickly rinse the soap letting all my stress drain away. I turn the shower off, grab my towel and gently blot my body dry. I quickly put on my tank top and black shorts. I gather my belongings off the bathroom floor to put them into my hamper. I open the bathroom door; Damon is lying on top of my cover with his shoes off, looking at the T.V. I walk to my dresser to put deodorant underneath my arms and behind my ear, so it does not smell like stank cheese. I sat on the side of my bed to rub lotion on my body. "Girl. You still do the same routine every night before you go to bed." I put the lotion container on the dresser, "Well, do you remember the next routine?"

Damon smiled as I laid next to him in bed. "I sure do," he cut the lights and T.V. off, turning on my little clock radio to the jazz channel. He wrapped his arms around my body, holding me passionately. "I miss these nights, Shanel,"

I sigh, "Yeah, me too." We just lay in the dark, relaxing with the sound of saxophones echoing in my bedroom, until his cell phone rang. "Damn! Don't answer that phone." He chuckles, "I have to take this call. It's my mom's, hey, Mom, what do you need?"

She cries, "I need a ride home; my transmission went out on me again."

"Okay, Mom, calm down. I'll be there in twenty minutes. We are going to have to cut this short tonight. My mom's car broke down again at her job." Damon cut on the lamp, getting out of bed, putting on his shoes. I put on my slides, following downstairs behind him as he walks to the front door, "Damn, look at all those roaches on the floor."

I sigh, "I know I'll sweep them up; oh yeah, speaking of cars, what will you do with my car Damon?"

Opening the front door, he laughs, "That is not a car. That is a bomb on wheels waiting to explode,"

I said, "That's okay, but that car you call a bomb got me back and forth to work."

He laughs, "All right, get some sleep; you have a big day ahead of you."

"Oh, Damon, I meant to ask you earlier, which cousin is picking your son and me up?"

He replied, "My cousin Dee,"

My smile quickly fades, "Oh hell Nah, you know damn well I don't like your lazy ass cousin. Did his ass get a job?" we stand in the doorway talking, "Nah, he still staying with his mama controlling everything that's not his,"

I sigh with my arms folded, shaking my head, ", why don't you and your family get together and kick his ass out? He would have no choice but to get a job."

Damon rubs his head, looking around, making sure nobody runs up on him, "I hear what you are trying to say, but It's not that easy," I shake my head, "Is your auntie scared of your cousin Dee?"

He said, "I don't know," I suck my teeth, "I can't stand your cousin; he better not come at me the wrong way either." "Shanel, chill the hell out. He is doing me a favor," said Damon I roll my eyes, "He needs to do his mama a favor and find himself a job. He needs to stop living off her. Damon leans up against the side of the wall. "What happened to your cousin anyway? I thought he wanted to be a dentist?"

Damon sighed, "He was messing around with those trifling hood rats that didn't have his best interest," I said, "Well, he needs to get over that crap; that was his fault for letting those hood rats bring him down. I can't stand a sorry-ass man."

Damon frowns, "Me either, now lock up," His phone vibrates in his pocket, and he answers the phone, "What's good, cuz? Hold on,"

"All right, man."

He smiles, "This Dee. I will talk to you later,"

"Alright, good night," I locked my door and swept up the dead roaches on the floor.

It is two forty-five in the morning. I need to set my alarm clock for seven a.m. to pick up Josh from Ms. Waters' house.

Chapter 6

I woke up at six-thirty in the morning only to get about three hours of sleep. It's Sunday, but I will not be going to church. I don't feel like dealing with my sisters. I should never have invited them to my church. Now I must find another church. Why do I feel moist between my legs? Dang, I came on my period. Thank goodness I didn't stain my sheets. I jumped into the shower and accidentally turned on the cold water instead of the hot water. I screamed so loud, gee whiz! I fix the temperature of the water to a lukewarm, much better. I quickly showered because I cannot afford any sky-high water bill. I wrapped my towel around my body and washed out my blooded underwear in the sink. I hung them up on the towel rack to dry. I glance at the clock while I'm drying off. It's almost seven a.m. I rush to get dressed to pick up my son from Ms. Waters' house. I slip on my slides and walk downstairs, seeing more dead roaches on the floor. Damn. I grab the broom sweeping up a dustpan full of roaches. I empty them in the trash and wash my hands. My phone vibrates on the table. It's probably Ms. Waters. Let me check my phone just to make sure. It was just a message alert. Damn, I have six voicemails from Sharon Jada, and Melissa. Gees, I'm not dealing with these ignorant heifers today. I set my cell phone on the table and open up my curtain before leaving to get my son. It's such a beautiful day. Damn, I spoke too soon again. There are seven police cars across the street from Ms. Water's townhouse. My heart beats extra fast as I open my door, jogging toward Ms. Waters, "Hey Shanel, Josh, your mama here!" Josh came running behind her old wore out wooden gate, "Hey, mama, I missed you." I hug my son, "Go back inside Ms. Waters' house,"

"Yes ma'am," said Josh.

I asked, "What happened over there?"

She replied, "Domestic violence that turned to murder,"

I was shocked, "What? Are you serious?"

"Yeah, baby, I heard screaming around six a.m. this morning. Some people get scared and don't do anything. I was not going to have that on my conscience, so I called the damn police, baby."

"You did right, Ms. Waters," we continue standing outside, watching all the commotion across the street. People in the neighborhood were coming out trying to see and talking amongst each other, "By the way, Josh already ate breakfast." Ms. Waters taps me on the arm, "Look at the hypocrite hippo," I glance toward my townhouse and see Gina in church clothes. She waves, "Good morning, Ms. Waters and Shanel," I wave, "Morning, Gina." Ms. Waters smiles, "Morning, baby. I see you on your way to church?" Gina smiles, "Yes, ma'am, I need that word to start my week off right," Ms. Waters chuckles, "Bring me back a CD."

Gina replied with a big Kool-Aid smile, "Yes, ma'am," Gina and her husband got into the car and drove off. Ms. Water frowns as she digs in her chest to take out her weed and lighter. "I promise Gina is the biggest hypocrite in the world." I began laughing as Ms. Waters lit her marijuana and ran her mouth, "Shanel, you know I'm right. Her ass is always playing spades, drinking beer, and smoking weed every day. Gina is a wolf in sheep's clothing."

I shake my head at Ms. Waters as she takes a long puff on her weed, "I thought you and Gina were close?" Ms. Waters gave me that evil look, "Honey, trust me, the same thing I am telling you I already told Gina and her husband to their face. Thank the Lord; she cannot have children because those kids would be fucked up by now." Ms. Waters raises her hands to the heavens with her weed on the side of her mouth. I chuckle, "I hate to hear what you say about me when I'm not around," Ms. Waters taps me on the shoulder, "Honey, please, I pray for you to get up on your feet and stop letting your family bring you down. You are a strong woman, but you don't see it, Shanel. You are too busy arguing with your family that you can see what God is about to do in your life. Stop moping around your house, complaining to God about what you don't have, and be grateful for what you do have. God does not like to hear you complaining; he wants to hear praises."

I sigh, "I hear you, Ms. Waters."

She smiles, "Listen to God and do what he says, Shanel. I'll tell you one thing: God will change Damon around, and you two will get married. That boy loves you; anybody can see that, Shanel. You just don't want to accept it. Damon is good-looking. Do you know how often Gina and her sister have tried to get with him?"

I frowned, "How do you know?"

"Hold up, suga, let me get this last good puff before I answer that," I had to laugh at Ms. Waters, "Now, this herb right here is natural and good for you. It helps me with my chronic pain. What were we talking about?"

I said, "Um, Gina and her sister are pushing up on Damon,"

Ms. Waters rubs her hair, "oh yeah, Damon talks to me about everything,"

I hold my head down, "I didn't know that" Ms. Waters takes my hand, "Baby, trust and believe. Damon's heart has your name on it, and that's all I need to say about that matter. So, are you excited about leaving out the ghetto?"

I shrug my shoulders, "I'm not sure." Ms. Waters gave me the crazies look I ever saw, "I may be high, but what the hell do you mean you're not sure? Girl, please, I'll be praising God for getting me out of this awful ass place." I tap Ms. Waters, "Lord, they finally bringing the body out. They have the woman in handcuffs," said Ms. Waters. We look on as they put the body in the ambulance. "She killed that man; he really must have driven her over the edge," I said.

Ms. Waters added, "And on the Lord's Day."

I said, "I thought every day was Lord's Day." She said, "It is, baby, but it's Sunday, honey, church day,"

I laugh, "You a mess Ms. Waters.

Ms. Waters said, ", you better praise the lord that you are leaving this awful place."

I sigh, "Easy said than done. Do you know how many times I have had a good life, then it gets snatched away from me for some odd reason? It is like a cycle that won't stop Ms. Waters.

She said, "Honey, you need to get on your knees and pray to God about it."

"I do Ms. Waters,"

"Then let it go, and do not pick it back up. Let God straighten it out for you. Now you go and start packing up; I need to go and clear my glaucoma so I can feel better."

"Don't smoke too much, Ms. Waters,"

"Oh honey, please, it is natural. It does not kill you. It's the ones that are lace that kill you. I will send Josh out," Ms. Waters walks to her townhouse. I watched the police pass by with the young lady in the back of the police car with her head down. Gina's sister, Lena, is walking toward the street crub. She asked, "Shanel, what the hell happened?"

I said, "Domestic Violence that turned deadly."

She frowns, "Damn, that's sad,"

Josh comes running toward me, "You ready to go home?"

"Yes, ma'am," We crossed the street and went inside my townhouse. I flop on my comfort zone couch, "mama your phone is ringing,"

I said, "Let it ring, if it's important they will call my house phone.," his face lit up when he saw his dad's name on the phone, "It's my daddy."

I said, "Answer the phone,"

Josh is excited, "Hey, Daddy,"

"Hey, little man, let me speak to your mother," Josh hands me the phone and sits beside me on the sofa.

"Hello,"

He asked, "Are you and Josh ready?"

I smile, "Yes, Damon,"

He said, "Change of plans. I'm picking you up. I don't know where my cousin is this morning. They said he left with a woman from the club last night, so it's no telling where the hell he's at."

I frown, shaking my head, "Your cousin is not thinking about you. He was too busy shacked up with some gullible ass woman. What time are you coming through?"

He said, "Uh, I should be there in five to ten minutes," "Good, I should be finished packing me and Josh's clothes,"

He said, "Leave all that. I'm going to take y'all shopping,"

Josh taps my arm, "Mama, somebody is knocking at the door," I get up from my comfort zone couch, "I'll see you when you get here. I hang up my phone and open the door, "I cut my eyes, "Melissa?" She forces herself into my townhouse, "Jada told me how you treated her," she sat down on my comfort zone couch as I closed my front door, "Uh, that was two weeks ago, you Jada bodyguard now?" I asked.

I sat in the chair across from Melissa; she said, "No, I'm just a concerned cousin. Your sister didn't even go to church today because of you. l,"

I have a blank expression, "I don't care; I didn't make her stay home from church. That was her choice."

Melissa glares at me, "Your sister is a wreck, and Sharon is not far behind her,"

I said, "Girl, please, I'm not in the mood for your negative energy,"

Melissa sighed, "I'm not negative; I'm trying to bring positivity into the equation." I throw my hands up to the heavens, "Well, you can take all this so call positive energy to Jada and Sharon since they supposed to be such nervous wrecks,"

She frowns, "don't make me beat your ass,"

I scoff, "I know you did lose your mind coming into my house, threatening to lay hands on me in front of my son."

Melissa backs down into the couch, "All I'm saying…" I cut her off, "You ain't say nothing worth my damn time,"

She heavily sighs, ", all I'm trying to say is you can't blame your sisters for how your daddy treated you."

I get up from my chair and Melissa flinches. I chuckle as I walk to the kitchen to get my son a fruit snack out of the cabinet. Melissa's eyes stayed piercing on me. She didn't know what to expect from me. I hand Josh his fruit snack; he said, "Thank you, Mom,"

I look in Melissa's direction leaning on the back chair. "Let me ask you a question, Melissa; why haven't you taken the time to invite me over to your apartment?"

she paused, "Huh?"

"I didn't stutter,"

She replied, "Because you didn't ask me,"

I glared at her rubbing through my hair. I asked, "Why do I have to ask when you just freely show your ass up at my townhouse. Something wrong with that picture."

Josh sees his dad walking up, "Mommy, Daddy here,"

I said, "Go outside with your daddy,"

Melissa looks out the window, "Shanel please understand, it's not about you,"

I laugh, "Girl, please, you, Sharon, and Jada sound like a broken ass record. You can't fix a record once it broke, and you can fix this problem."

Melissa frowns, "You are comparing us to a broken record?"

I had to laugh at Melissa's dumb ass, "Chile, for you to have a college degree, you are one dumb heifer. You need to ask for a refund."

Damon and Josh walk in the front door before Melissa could respond. Damon sees the expression on my face, and he asks, "Is everything all right, Shanel?"

I replied, "Yes, I'm fine,"

Damon walked toward me and asked, "How are you, Melissa?"

She smiles, "You're still fine as hell, but I am doing okay. You just need to talk some sense into Shanel's head,"

Damon motioned Josh to go upstairs, and he sat down in the chair I was leaning on, "What's wrong?" asked Damon, "Shanel is worried about the wrong thing," I was going to say something, but Damon gestured for me to chill. I grabbed a chair from the kitchen and sat beside him.

"Like what?" asked Damon.

Melissa sighed, "Just talk to her,"

He replied, "I can't talk to her if I don't know what the problem is at hand,"

Melissa said, "She needs to treat her sister with respect. They tried their best to help Shanel,"

Damon is pissed, trying to keep his composure, "Hold up Melissa, that respect goes both ways, and as far as you all trying to help Shanel, that's a fucking overstatement."

Melissa gets an attitude, "We do respect and try to help Shanel, ass."

Damon flexes his jaw muscle in anger, pointing toward Melissa making his point, "No, Melissa, you know damn well that Sharon and Jada treat Shanel, who is a grown woman, like a damn child. All of y'all feel that Shanel is beneath you because of her current situation.

Melissa said, "That's because my cousin acts childish. Now, as far as her situation goes, she is beneath us. Look how the hell she's living. She chose to live like this and then wants to get angry and blame the family for her damn failures."

Damon gestures his hand in Melissa's direction, "The perfect example. See how you are coming over to Shanel's townhouse talking shit about her right in front of her face? How the hell are you helping her? You don't have a fucking clue what's going on in Shanel's life. You are going on the shit that you heard from her sister and whoever else that got something negative to say about Shanel."

She points in my direction, "They are just trying to help her, Damon,"

He sharply sighs, shaking his head, "bullshit! If you believe that, then you waste all that college education on an empty ass brain. Melissa, bringing negative energy into somebody's space and belittling them; it's not helping. It's tearing them down."

Melissa scoffs, "Whatever, Sharon and Jada are nice people. Too bad Shanel didn't inherit that quality," I see Damon Jaws clutching, so I jump in the conversation, "Melissa, you can do me a favor and get the hell out before I throw your ass out."

She gets up from the sofa, "You make me sick bitch. I will call your mama so she can talk some sense into that thick skull you call a brain."

I open the door, "Just wait, Shanel. I'm going to call your sisters too. We will be back." Damon gets up from the chair, and walks to the door, shouting, "Go ahead, you'll be here by your damn self! He slammed the door in her face.

Damon kicked the chair over; he shouted, "Your family is fucking toxic!" I nod in agreement; He paces back and forth, slowly calming himself down. He asked, "Shanel, are you ready to go?" I looked out the window; I said, "She is still out there, Damon." His face changed from fine wine to Neo Brown mode from New Jack City. He said, "Look at my face. I don't give a damn, she, not the fucking police, now let's go." I quickly ran upstairs to grab my bag with all my relevant documents and get Josh. We walked back downstairs; he said, "I thought I told you to leave all that shit behind. I will get a new bag. Didn't I tell you I'll take care of you and Josh," I said, "Yes, you did, but these are my important papers,"

He said, "Well, before you step foot into your new townhome, you going to shake that bag out to make sure no roaches are hiding in the cracks," said Damon.

 I laugh, "Whatever, I'm so glad to be leaving this place."

"Me too," said Josh,

Damon and I chuckle, "I'll come back and take care of all this mess. Hell, all you have is a couch, chair, and dining table with two chairs that should have been in the dumpster a long time ago."

I chuckle, "You call it a mess, but it served its purpose. What are you going to do with my nineteen-seventy-thirteenth-inch TV?"

He laughs, "The dumpster, hell, they should have stolen that when they took the one in the living room.

I asked, "What about our beds and dresser?"

Damon said, "The dumpster. Now let's go before your sisters show up." We leave the townhouse, and Damon locks the door behind us. Melissa, on the phone, looking in our direction, Lena smiles when she sees Damon; she walks over to him, trying to get a hug. He pushes her away, and she frowns. Lena said, "I know damn well you not tripping on me? Shanel ain't shit, I will beat your baby mama down in front of you and your son nigga."

Melissa walks over to me, asking, "Shanel, where are you going?" Sharon and Jada are on their way over here."

I said, "I don't care because I'm not going to be here."

Damon shouted, "Shanel, you and my son, get in the car now!" Lena grabs Damon by the arm, "What is wrong with you? Why are you acting shady toward me? I am not Gina!" she raises her voice, making sure I heard her. "Damon, did you tell your baby mama that you have been all up in me? Damon pushes Lena out of the way. She grabs his shirt trying to rip it off him. Lena shouts, "You're not leaving, nigga!" Damon grabs her by the arm and whispers in Lean ear, "If you don't stop showing your ass out in front of my son and let loose my shirt, I will tell Gina you slept with her husband on her birthday in her bed." Damon walks away from Lena and gets in his car. He pulls off before Lena, and Melissa could start anything else with us. They were so pissed they spat at the car and flicked us off. Damon scoffs, "Crazy hood rats." He cut down the side road so he wouldn't bump into my sisters, "Good riddance to negative energy," said Damon. I didn't even question him about the Lena incident. Ms. Waters had already filled me in on the tea.

Sharon and Jada pulled up eight mins later at Shanel's townhouse. Melissa walks to the car, "You just missed them, "you all need to check Shanel's attitude for real. I almost beat her ass." Sharon shakes her head in agreement, "I told you she was rude. That's why she is going through so much now." Melissa glances toward the streets, "Who is this old ass lady walking over here?"

"I don't know," said Sharon.

Lena chuckles, "That's Ms. Waters, the crazy busybody neighborhood mom. I'm gone. I don't have time to be dealing with her ass today."

"Hello, girls, I'm Ms. Waters," They all said hello in unison." Ms. Waters smokes her weed sizing the girls up. "What brings y'all to the ghetto?"

"None of your business," said Melissa,

Ms. Waters takes a long puff before responding, "Do you know who I am?"

Melissa chuckles, "The ghetto busybody?"

Ms. Waters frowns, "No, you better watch yourself,"

Melissa's chuckles fade, "What are you going to do, old lady?" Ms. Waters finish smoking her weed, pointing her finger at Melissa, "I'll whip your ass, little girl,"

Melissa runs up to Ms. Waters, "Little girl! I am a grown woman,"

Ms. Waters chuckles, "You tell me you a grown woman, but you come over to Shanel's townhouse acting like snotty nose spoil bitches, putting her down every chance you all get."

Sharon said, "Old lady, you don't know anything about Shanel,"

Ms. Waters replied, "I'll tell you this I'm more family than y'all so call sisters are, you dirty hood rats."

"Old lady, you wanna get your ass beat," said Sharon.

"She laughs, "You lay one hand on me and watch this neighborhood whip y'all ass," Jada grabs Sharon and Melissa, "Let's go," Lena sitting on the porch laughing, drinking a beer.

Ms. Waters yells, "That's right; you all better leave and don't come back over here bothering Shanel no more! You all some trifling stuck-up bitches!"

Sharon gasped, "That old sack of bones just called us out our name."

Jada frowns, "Forget that old lady; our main concern is Shanel right now. Just get in the car so that we can go. "They finally get in the car, and Sharon calls her sister. "It went straight to voice mail,"

Sharon leaves a message. Melissa gets out of Jada's car, "I'll ride behind y'all," Jada waits for Melissa to get in her car, "Look at that old sack of bones. You should run her ass over Jada," Jada chuckles, "I'm not going to jail over her ignorant ass," They pulled out of the parking lot, giving Ms. Waters the finger. Ms. Waters shouts, "Curse those bitches now!"

Chapter 7

Damon and I drove in silence to my townhome. When we pulled up to the security gate, I began smiling, "Dang, these are nice," Damon punched in the security code, and he said, "I know, right," The gates open we drive in. I could not stop smiling. My cheeks hurt, and I asked, "How much did this set you back, Damon?" He smiles, "Don't worry about that. All you need to know is that I paid for it and it's all yours. That's it, don't ask me no more questions." I kept pinching my arm to make sure I wasn't dreaming. I asked, "Are you sure these are townhomes? They look like homes," Damon pulls up in the driveway, "Yes, it has four bedrooms," I sit in the car in amazement.

Damon cuts off the vehicle, "Shanel are you going to sit in the car or go inside to see your new townhome?" My smile faded, "I want to see my new room," said Josh. My heart begins pounding extra fast, and the palms of my hand start sweating. Damon and Josh got out of the car. He asked, "Shanel, are you coming?" My eyes begin tearing up; I start talking to the Lord. Is this mine? I can't say for sure yet, lord. You know my history, Lord, every time something good happens to me, it gets…"

Damon opens my car door, "Shanel, we are waiting for you. Are you okay?"

I nod yes, "Well, come on," He helps me out the car, taking my hand, walking me up the stairs; Damon said, "Okay, Josh, are you ready to see your new home?" Josh jumps up and down, "Yes, Daddy, hurry up, please, please, please, Daddy!" Damon opens the door, and Josh runs inside the townhome. My eyes grew the size of a golf ball. I asked, "Oh my goodness, are you serious? Are you sure this is Josh and my townhome?” I sigh, looking around my townhome, “Yes, Shanel, you see, I already furnished your townhome.”

I smile, “Oh my goodness, Damon, this is the same sofa I told you about two years ago.”

I flop down letting my hand caress the sofa. Damon said, “Trust me, trying to find this sofa was not easy either. Hell, it was hard to find your sky blue and fuchsia pillows, but I did it.”

I walk up to Damon and give him a huge hug, “Thank you,”

He embraced my hug, “You welcome,”

Josh runs downstairs into the living room with excitement. “Daddy, I like my room, Mommy. Come and see my room.” I run behind Josh upstairs, “Mommy, look at you and daddy,” I shake my head, chuckling, “Oh my goodness, Damon, where did you find that picture of me?” he walks into Josh's bedroom, “Oh, I went through my old photo album and had my uncle’s girlfriend paint that into a mural,”

Josh said, “Mommy, I didn’t know you were a cheerleader,” I gazed at the mural, “Yeah, baby, many years ago.” Josh jumps on the bed, “Look at daddy dunking’ the basketball,” I smile, “I see, baby,”

Josh jumps off the bed, running to his TV, “Mommy, look, I have a computer. I like my room. Look at all the books that Daddy bought me.” I glance at Damon, then back at Josh, “Baby, I’m so happy for you, but I love that cheerleader on the wall. She is gorgeous.” Damon and I left Josh in his room to enjoy. Damon takes my hand, “Where are we going?” He opens the door to my bedroom, “Damon, oh my goodness, it’s purple and fuchsia, my favorite colors. I like it, Damon. This is too much,”

He said, "No, it's not Shanel,"

I smile, "I'm happy, but I'm not if that makes sense." Damon's smiles fade away, "What the fuck did you just say?" I sat on the bed, "Don't get upset. I'm grateful, but I'm scared, Damon." he sighed, leaning against the bedroom door, "Why Shanel?" I heavily sigh, "You know, every time I get something, I'm always losing it, having to start all over from scratch. I'm tired of that cycle."

Damon said, "Not this time Shanel,"

I asked, "How you know, Damon?" he walked over to me, kneeling on the floor, holding my hand, "Look, after Josh was born, I was angry when your mama took it upon herself to name my only son. That shit hurt, I start dipping out on you with different girls and leave you alone. I got a job and gave you a little money, but you were still struggling. Shanel, it's time for you to rest because, through all my transgression, you took care of our son. Shanel, when you lost your salary job, you still made provisions. You did not give up on life, and you got a minimum-wage job. You kept your head up even when your sisters and cousin belittled you. I have so much respect for the mother of my child." Damon wiped my tears away, shaking his head; he said, "Sharon is the worst out of Jada and Melissa. She just doesn't know the guy she is dating is doing mind control on her ass. He is going to jack her ass up. Besides, you don't have to worry about them anymore unless you bring them back into your life. Then that's on you."

I frown, "oh, trust me, that's not happening, Damon,"

"Well, then, you don't have to worry about anything. Unlike my trifling brothers, Dontae, who thinks he's a badass carrying around an unloaded gun, he a straight-up pussy. He's a weak-minded bastard that can't control his women. They walk all over his ass, and then when he gets in trouble, he wants to call everybody to rescue his sorry ass." I laugh as Damon continues talking about his brothers. He gets off his knees, limping to the chair next to my bed, "Now my brother Dondre he's just a stupid ass. He talks trash to people smaller than him. He makes women buy him clothes and give him money."

I asked, "Are you serious?"

"Yes, Shanel, that is why I didn't bring you around, my brothers. Then there is my mama, well, you know how she takes up for my brothers. She is scared to tell my brothers how she feels, but she will go off on me when they make her angry. I don't say anything because when I moved back to California, my mama is going to have to handle their asses."

I had a shocked expression on my face. I asked, "So you are making California your permanent home?"

He replied, "Yeah, I can't stay in Atlanta anymore. I need to get the hell out of here. If I continue to live here, I'll end up in jail for drugs or killing my brothers."

I sigh, "That's how I feel about my sisters and Melissa."

"Well, look at this as a new beginning for you and Josh. You don't have to be around your family; this community is gated." Said Damon.

I smiled, "I know,"

"You can even look for a new church. My cousin told me about this non-domination church his girlfriend attends. I will get you the information before I leave on Wednesday." Said Damon.

I said, "Okay, but for now, I think I'll watch church via T.V. for a while."

"I'm going to have to start quickly on your old townhouse and get things squared away. I'll be putting money in your account." Said, Damon

I smiled, "Okay, how much do you get paid, Damon?"

He laughs, "Just say that this townhome and the furniture didn't put a dent in my pocket."

"Wow! Damon," I lay down in the bed with a big smile on my face. "So, you happy with everything?" asked Damon

I said, "Yeah, I'm excited."

Damon said, "I want you and Josh to be able to live life to the fullest before you get old and gray," I threw the decorative pillow from the bed at Damon, "Shut up, you are not funny,"

He said, "For real, Shanel, I want you to stop stressing about the past and live for the future. Speaking of the future, I need to call my boy. Damon reached into his back jeans pocket to retrieve his phone. "Damn, I forgot to take my phone off silent," he looks through his cell phone, "my mom has been blowing up my phone," Damon returns his mom's call," He puts his blue tooth on, and she answers on the first ring, "Damon where are you?" "Why Mama?" she breathes heavily through the phone, "I have some bad news," Damon rubs his head, "Mama, what is it?" her voice begins to crack, "Dee was killed this morning," Damon jumps up from the chair, "Repeat that mama," Damon fight back his tears, "Mama I just talked to him early Sunday morning. What happen?" Damon's mom responded with a soft unhappy voice, "He met some girl at the club and went home with her. They got into an argument, and she shot Dee in the head, neck, and chest. Your auntie had to go identify his body this morning." Damon walks out of the room. I get out the bed to follow him downstairs in the living room, "Damn, did they lock her ass up," his mama begins to cry on the phone, "I believe so. I need to go. This is just too painful to talk about." Damon hangs up with his mama. He looks at me with sad droopy eyes, "What's wrong, Damon," he walks toward me and hugs me tight, "My cousin Dee was killed this morning," my heart drops to my stomach, "I am so sorry. Damon, how did he die?"

Damon pulled away from me, he flopped on the sofa, trying to fight his tears, but they finally won, streaming down his face, "It was domestic violence," I sat next to Damon, "Damn, that's two killings in one day, somebody was killed in my old neighborhood this morning. Ms. Waters heard screaming and called the police." Damon gets up from the sofa, "I need to go meet up with my family."

"Yeah, your family needs you right now," he takes the keys and one hundred dollars in twenty out of his pocket, putting it in my hand. "You may want to order out tonight. I'm going to give Ms. Waters the rest of the food from the refrigerator and cabinets. I'll be back later tonight." I walk Damon out the front door; he slowly walks down the stairs getting into his car. I close the door as he backs out of the driveway. Lord, I'm so sorry for talking ill against his cousin Dee. I feel guilty; Lord forgive me. Josh walks downstairs, calling for his dad. "Mommy, where is Daddy?"

"He had to leave; he'll be back later tonight." Josh frowned. I said, "Come here and give me a hug," he slowly walked to me with his mouth poked out. "Mommy loves you,"

Josh said, "I love you to mommy, I'm glad you are happy again mommy, Jesus took care of you," my eyes began to water up, "Yes, he did. I wasn't expecting this, baby. So, what do you want to eat for lunch Josh?" he smiles, "Cheese Pizza,"

I said, "Okay, one cheese pizza and one order of chicken wings,"

"Thank you, Mommy. I'm going back upstairs to read the brand-new books that Daddy bought me," said Josh. I smile, watching my son walk upstairs.

Chapter 8

I don't know what to do with myself. I am so used to my sisters popping up over my townhouse unannounced, putting me down every chance they get. Jesus, I don't know how to feel or act right now. I'm so confused; everything happened so fast. My phone rings. I glance at the number. I sigh before answering, "Hello, Mother."

"Where the hell you at?" asked Ms. Howard

I asked, "Why?"

Ms. Howard is fussing, "Because your sisters are worried about you,"
I replied in a calm tone, "I'm a grown woman who can take care of myself," Ms. Howard chuckles, "Since when have you been able to take care of yourself, Shanel? Your ass is shacking up with Damon again." I shake my head, looking toward the ceiling in my new townhome, "It's none of your business what I'm doing. I don't have to tell you anything, mama."

Ms. Howard screams through the phone, "Ugh, girl, you better be lucky. I can't come through the phone and beat your ass!"

I smirk, "You gotta catch me first."

"Girl! You a rotten evil ass seed. I should have aborted your ass a long time ago. My fucking life would have been a whole lot better than what it is now." said Ms. Howard

I said, "Mama, I'm so used to you telling me how you feel that it doesn't even phase me anymore. I'm sorry that your only child brought you so much pain in your life, mama, but I didn't ask to be here."

Ms. Howard said, "You are a curse from the devil, you evil bitch! I HATE YOU, SHANEL! My eyes water up, "Mama, I know you didn't want me when I was a baby. Hell, you and Daddy disowned me. You never taught me anything. I had to learn from my teachers how to care for myself." Ms. Howard sucks her teeth, "Shanel. I don't regret a damn thing, so don't be trying to make me feel guilty."

I said, "Mama, I'm not going to worry about you anymore. This will be our last conversation over the phone,"

Ms. Howard chuckles, "I don't care, Shanel. You not hurting me."

I sigh, "I know mama. I thank the Lord for Ms. Waters. She has been more of a grandmother to Josh than you were,"

Ms. Howard laughs, "That old drunk-ass woman who is always smoking weed? Girl, please, you better watch out for her. She isn't who you think she is, Shanel. Just because I don't like your ass, I have unconditional love for my grandson."

I sigh, "Mama, you are sick; you don't know how to love nobody because you don't love yourself." Ms. Howard becomes silent on the phone. "Mama, I want to thank you for preparing me for a huge blessing." Ms. Howard shouted, "A blessing, girl. God doesn't like you. I have been telling you that all your life. That's why you go through so much. Shanel, do your family a favor and just commit suicide so we all can get rid of your evil ass." My heart nearly drops to my stomach, "I'm not going to give you the satisfaction,"

"Shanel, you worthless along with your sorry-ass baby daddy. He may be fine, but he ain't shit."

I shook my head; I said, "Mama, go ahead and continue to belittle me. It seems to make you happy,"

Ms. Howard said, "The only thing I truly do regret is not getting that damn abortion. I should have listened to your daddy, but no, my dumb ass kept you hoping your daddy would change his mind about you."

"Mama, I'm here because it is God's will, not yours or Daddy. I can either hold a grudge or forgive."

Ms. Howard shout through the phone, "Don't go preaching that Bible shit to me!" I hear my doorbell.

I said, "You are so full of hate, mama; you have a good life. The delivery guy is at the door," I hung up the phone before my mama could respond. I walk to the door, "who is it?"

"Great Time Pizza," said a young lady who sounded like a little girl. I open the door to a young husky blonde girl with a huge smile, "Hi, my son has been waiting for you."

She smiles as she hands me the receipt. I gave her forty dollars; meanwhile, my cell phone continuously ringing. I watch her count my money to ensure she gives me my correct change. She hands me my change, pizza, and chicken wings, "You have a wonderful day." Said the young lady. I close the door and walk to the kitchen. Josh comes downstairs, "Mommy, is that the pizza?"

I replied, "Yes, it is," I looked in the cabinet for a plate and saw paper plates with a note. "You must pick your China patterns out. In the meantime, here are paper plates." I laugh, Damon is a nut. I gave Josh a large slice of cheese pizza with four chicken wings. "Mommy, can I eat in my room at my table?"

I smiled, "Yes, but you better not make a mess,"

"Yes, ma'am," Josh walks upstairs with his plate in his hand like a big boy. I walk to my phone to see who is blowing up my cell phone; it's my mother. Sorry mama, I'm done with you.

Chapter 9

Sharon, Jada, and Melissa are parked back in front of Shanel's old townhouse, waiting for her to come home, "Y'all keep an eye out for that old bag of bones across the street while I'm on the phone with Ms. Howard." said Sharon, Jada, and Melissa both nodded, looking out for Ms. Waters. Ms. Howard is shouting on the phone to Sharon, "That evil rotten seed you call your sister has no respect. I hate that girl so much, Sharon. She is not my daughter. I wish she were dead." Sharon frowns, "Oh no, Ms. Howard, that is a cruel thing to say about your daughter. I see why Shanel always has her caution flags up." Ms. Howard raises her voice, "Sharon, don't let Shanel suck you into her manipulation. Let me talk to Jada and Melissa; I need one of their boys to help me order a hit on Shanel."

Sharon reaches for her chest, "Oh my goodness, Ms. Howard, do not say that Shanel is your daughter and my sister,"

Ms. Howard replied, "Whatever. She does not suppose to disrespect her mama on the phone."

Sharon asked, "How did Shanel disrespect you?"

She said, "For one, she trying to preach to me about the bible; I know what the damn bible says; I'm no damn child." Sharon tries to keep from laughing, "I thought she did something terrible," she shouts through the phone, "she did; she also hung up in my damn face!"

"Okay, Ms. Howard, you need to calm down. Just don't do anything that's going to land you in jail. I will talk to you later." Sharon hangs up shaking her head, "Oh my goodness, lord, Ms. Howard is one crazy lady," said Sharon.

"What happened?" asked Jada.

Sharon frown, "Girl, she is talking about putting a hit on Shanel,"

Melissa said, "That is one wacky lady; she needs to be locked up in somebody's mental institute,"

Jada asked, "What time is it??"

Sharon responded sarcastically, "Duh, it's after two. The clock is right in front of your face, heifer," Melissa sighed, "Let's go; Shanel isn't coming back home no time soon. I'm hungry; let's go get something to eat."

"I'm not hungry," said Sharon. Jada nodded in agreement. Melissa became irritated, "Damn, I shoulda stayed home."

"Chill the hell out, Melissa. We need to focus on Shanel right now," said Sharon.

Melissa cut her eyes at Sharon, "Why she was damn well rude to me along with her sorry-ass baby daddy."

"Stop it, you two, I have a lot on my mind," said Jada.

Sharon asked, "Like what, Jada?"

She sighs, "Well, I feel bad for Shanel?"

Sharon and Melissa gave Jada a look of confusion before Sharon responded, "Why? She put herself through all this hell,"

"No, she didn't. How would you feel if Daddy disowned you at birth because you weren't a boy? Then her crazy ass mama didn't even take the time to love or raise her properly. Whether or not you'll agree, Shanel has been through hell. We were lucky to have our daddy and mother care for us. Think about it; if we were in Shanel's shoes, we would probably be feeling the same way she feels toward her family. We left her alone to suffer and tear her down."

Sharon is annoyed with her sister, "Oh please, Jada, everything Shanel is going through, she deserves it. Daddy told me how rude Shanel was to him."

Jada glares at her sister, "Well, Daddy is a liar."

Sharon frowns, pointing her finger at Jada, "I'm going to ask you to stop disrespecting Daddy, or I'm going to kick your ass out of my car."

Melissa suggested, "We can solve this issue right now; let's go, pay Uncle Darren a visit,"

"Good idea," said Sharon; she cranked up her Lexus and pulled out of Shanel's parking lot.

"Can we get something to eat on the way," asked Melissa,

Jada and Sharon both looked at Melissa, "no!"

"We need to get over to Daddy's house before he goes to his mason meeting," said Jada.

Sharon cut her eye, correcting her sister, "He goes on Wednesday night; today is Thursday." She was angry, "I just cannot believe you let Shanel brainwash your head about Daddy. Shanel has been a curse to Daddy."

Jada asked, "How? And why would you say that, Sharon?"

Sharon angrily hits the steering wheel, "Jada, are you kidding me? Don't you remember what Daddy said? As soon as Shanel was born, he lost his job. Then his brother, our uncle Mike was diagnosed with lung cancer, and to make matters worse, daddy mama died the day Shanel was born. Now that proves Shanel a curse."

"She sounds like a curse to me," said Melissa.

Jada shakes her head, "it's not Shanel fought,"

"Jada shut the hell up; we are going to talk to Daddy so he can set your ass straight once and for all. Girl, you are going to owe Daddy a huge-ass apology." Melissa nods her head in agreement with Sharon.

Jada clenches her jaws, "No, y'all heifers are going to be owing me an apology,"

"Can we please stop at burger king?" asked Melissa.

Sharon stares at Melissa in her rearview mirror with a straight attitude, "Girl, no, we're on a mission to prove Jada wrong; trust me, Daddy has a house full of food." Melissa pouts like a kid when they can't have their way. They drove in silence to their daddy's house.

Chapter 10

Ms. Howard is on the phone talking to Shanel's daddy, Darren, "Shelly, why are you calling me?" She replied in anger, "I'm sick and tired of that evil rotten seed we bought into the world."

""Well, we can do nothing about it, Shelly?"

"Yes, you can kill her ass off." Darren drops the phone in his lap with his mouth wide open; Shelly shouts through the phone, "Darren! Darren! Are you still there?" he slowly picks up the phone from his lap and puts it to his ear, "I'm here,"

"Well, did you hear what I said, Darren?"

He sighs, "Yes, Shelly; you can't be serious,"

Shelly replied with an angry, "I'm dead serious; you can poison her food or drink, so it won't link back to us,"

Darren scoffs, "What the hell, Shelly? She has a son, for heaven's sake."

Shelly mocks him, "Oh, now you wanna be a concerned parent? I don't give a damn about Shanel having a son; she can have that old pothead, drunken lady across the street from her, take care of Josh. Since she couldn't raise her child."

Darren raises his voice, "Damn! Just leave her alone, Shelly,"

She said, "I will leave her alone when Shanel is out of my life. Why is your phone echoing? I hope nobody isn't eavesdropping on our conversation,"

"Nah, Shelly, you're just being paranoid," she sucks her teeth. "Well, you remember, you called Shanel a curse,"

Darren scoffs, "For heaven's sake, I was young and stupid, Shelly."

"Don't you start getting soft on me, Darren?" He sighs, "You win, Shelly. I will meet with you tomorrow," Shelly hangs up; Darren sits back in his lazy boy with a blank expression. The doorbell rings: Darren's son comes downstairs to answer the door, he gets excited when he sees his sisters and cousin. "Hey Daryl," he hugs his sister and cousin, "daddy your daughters and niece are here,"

He shouts, "I'm in the den,"

Jada asked her brother, "How is college coming along?"

He frowns, "It's coming; Daddy is always on my ass," Sharon chuckles, "I know how you feel, trust me, Daddy don't play about getting a good education."

Daryl fidgets with his Jesus necklace, "Well, I need to study for my test tomorrow." Daryl runs back upstairs; they walk into the den. Sharon smiles, "Hey, Daddy," he grins, "Hey, my babies, how y'all doing this evening,"

"We are good," said Sharon. They sat on the sofa across from Darren; he asked, "What can I do for y'all?" Melissa answered, "Uncle Darren, is it okay if I can get something to eat." He nods, "help yourself," she walks into the kitchen. Sharon cut her eyes at Melissa, "I promise her mama mated with a pig; she a greedy heifer." They chuckle, "Be nice, Sharon. Now, what's on your mind?"

Sharon sighed, "we need to prove a point to Jada about our distance sibling Shanel,"

Darren's smile fades away, "What do you need to know about her?" he sits up in his recliner, "Daddy, can you please let Jada know how rude Shanel is and how she cured the family when she was born." Darren clears his throat, "You just said it, Sharon," Jada pulls an envelope out of her coach bag, "Daddy, can you explain this letter you wrote Shanel?" Jada gets up from the sofa handing him the letter. Darren reaches for his glasses off the table connected to his recliner. He glances over the letter; Darren sighs, tossing the letter back at Jada. "What's wrong, Daddy? Just tell Jada about Shanel so we can set her straight." Darren gets up from his recliner and walks outside to his deck. Melissa walks back into the den with a bag of chips. "What did I miss?" Sharon frowns, "We're waiting on Daddy to answer Jada's question about this letter." They follow him outside. "Daddy, we are waiting,"

He sighs heavily, "Why don't y'all girls just leave well enough alone."

Sharon got angry, "No, Daddy, you need to explain yourself to Jada right now."

"I can't, Sharon," Darren looks up to the heavens, then back at his daughters. She asked, "Why not, Daddy?"

Darren raises his voice at Sharon, "Because I put witchcraft on Shanel, so her life would be meaningless, that she would end her life. I turned my family, her mother, and you all against her; I wanted Shanel to feel the pain I endured when the doctor told me she was a girl instead of a boy. It has been eating away at me for years." Sharon grabs her chest, looking at her daddy in disgust, "I can't believe what I just heard coming out your mouth," Sharon cries, "I have been traumatized! I will never forgive you, Daddy." She walks back inside the house with tears coming down her face; Melissa follows behind her cousin to comfort her. Darren looks up to heaven, "I couldn't continue to live with the guilt for what I was doing to Shanel. That is why I stopped working against her almost three weeks ago. I wanted Shanel to have a chance to be happy and enjoy life with her son. When I saw Shanel driving that beat-up, raggedy, smokey Oldsmobile, I thought the car was going to blow up." Jada shakes her head, "Shanel must hate us; I didn't invite Shanel to my place of residence, because you said that the curse would come into my household and destroy me like Shanel. Now that I think about it, that curse could have jumped on me every time I was at her townhouse. Shit! I feel so damn stupid that I let you brainwash my head against my sister. I am shocked, and I'm hurt. Jada begins crying. I have so many emotions going on with me right now. Poor Sharon is heartbroken; she worshipped the ground you walked on. I need to go before I snap at you." Sharon walks back outside on the deck, in tears, with so much pain on her face. Sharon glances at Jada and then back at her daddy. Jada says, "Let's go,"

Sharon cries, "No, Jada! Daddy needs to pay for what the hell he did to us. You are a deacon in the church, a deacon, Daddy; I do not understand you." Darren sighed, "Well, I better tell y'all everything, Shelly, Ms. Howard to y'all wants me to kill Shanel." Sharon walks up to her daddy and slaps him in the face. "let's go, y'all," Jada screams at her sister, "Sharon! Did you not hear what Daddy just said?"

"Yes, I did. Now let's go," Darren walks back into the house while Sharon and Jada are fussing with each other, "I'm not leaving; we need to call the damn police on Daddy and Ms. Howard." Sharon wipes her face, "You call the police. I am leaving; come on, Melissa," Sharon and Melissa proceed to leave when they hear a gunshot; they stop in their tracks, looking at each other. Jada ran inside the house, and Daryl ran downstairs, "what happened?" They all went walking into the kitchen and saw their daddy, on the floor in a puddle of blood. They begin screaming, "Call 911!" Darryl reaches for the landline phone, dialing for help, "911, what's your emergency?" Daryl is breathing heavily, "Hello, my dad just shot himself!"

"Okay, what's your address?"

Daryl is speechless, "Uh…uh…"

"Sir, I need you to breathe and calm down." Said the operator.

Daryl's mouth is trembling, "My address is 55 Dale Oak Ln," The operator asked, "How old is the victim?"

Darryl is biting his lips, panicking, "Uh, he's fifty-six," The operator asked, "Okay, is he still breathing?"

Daryl shouts, "911 dispatcher wants to know if daddy is breathing?" Sharon shouts, "I don't know, Daryl; somebody needs to do CPR on Daddy and tell them to hurry up with paramedics. My daddy is losing a lot of blood!" Daryl continues talking to the 911 operator; Jada glares at her daddy; Melissa moves Jada out of the way so she can wipe up the blood. Sharon screams, "Wake up, daddy! Don't you die on me; wake up! I forgive you, Daddy. Help us, Lord!" Sharon is crying over her daddy, shaking him, "Wake up, please, wake up, Daddy."

Melissa throws the towel in a plastic bag and ties it up, then gets her phone to call her uncle Darren's wife at work, informing her what happened. Sharon cries, "Where is the ambulance? The hospital is only eight minutes away from the house." Jada is in shock, not able to move or say anything. "They're on the way," said Daryl." Jada runs outside on the deck, throwing up, while Sharon is screaming for her daddy to breathe, "Lord, don't take my daddy, please lord, he sorry for what he did. Please give him another chance, Lord. Please don't take my daddy." The ambulance and four police officers finally arrive at the house; the paramedics enter the house with a gurney. They see Darren on the floor, "What happened?" asked the first paramedics; Sharon shouted, "he shot himself!" The second paramedics begin attending Darren's womb. Sharon cries, "Could y'all please hurry the hell up? My daddy is losing a lot of blood!" the male paramedics continued wrapping Darren's head with bandages before responding, "Ma'am, please move out the way so we can do our job." Melissa moves Sharon to the side. "y'all just can't put my daddy on the damn gurney and wrap up his womb while wheeling him to the ambulance."

The lady paramedic shouted, "Ma'am, let us do our job! Okay, on my count, we will move him to the gurney on three, one…two…three. They put Darren on the gurney, rushing him to the ambulance. "I'm going to ride with Daddy to the hospital. Where is Jada?" asked Sharon?

"She outside on the deck vomiting," said Melissa. Sharon threw her hand up, "I'm gone," Daryl and Melissa walked behind Sharon, watching her get into the ambulance and ride off. One of the officers follows the ambulance to the hospital. The neighbors walk toward Daryl and Melissa, "What happened, Daryl?" said an older white gentleman,

Daryl replied, "My daddy shot himself,"

"Oh, how unfortunate. I'm going to keep your family in my prays." He walks away, shaking his head, notifying the other neighbors. Two officers are still in the house investigating the crime scene and taking pictures.

Melissa is in disbelief, "I can't believe Uncle Darren shot himself,"

Daryl frowns as he closes the front door, "I can. You don't know your uncle Darren," Melissa turns to Daryl, "Why would you say that?" before he could answer, Jada walks toward them with teary eyes, "What the hell just happened? I feel like I'm in a horror movie right now." Melissa comforts Jada, "Daddy is a damn coward; instead of facing his sin, he takes the easy way out. He's a weak, evil man." One of the two officers walked toward the foyer, interrupting the conversation, "I need to ask you three a couple of questions?" They all sigh at once, "sure said Jada,"

The officer asked, "What happened here today?"

Jada sighs heavily wiping her away tears, "My daddy shot himself?"

"Was he on any kind of medication?" asked the officer.

Jada replied, "I don't think so, Daryl, do you know if daddy was on medication?" He shakes his head, no. The second officer joins us in the foyer "Was your dad depressed about anything?" Jada glanced at her brother. He shrugs his shoulders, Jada said, "I don't recall officer.

All right, we will be in touch if we have any more questions." Said the officer. Daryl closed the door behind the officers, "I'm glad they have gone. Now, what set Daddy off to shoot himself?" asked Daryl. Jada looks at Melissa and then at her brother Daryl, "We were asking him questions about Shanel?" Daryl walks into the den. They followed behind him and sat down on the sofa, "I found a letter that Daddy was writing Shanel a week ago,"

Jada asked, "Where is it now?"

He said, "I sent it off to Shanel," he cleared his throat, "Um, sis, you should know Daddy made some changes to his will. He told my mother and me two weeks ago that if anything happens to him, we need to be strong and for me to finish school. My mama didn't take daddy's words seriously at the time." Jada shakes her head, "After all that just went down with Daddy, I don't feel sorry for him. Hell, I don't know how to feel right now."

Melissa is sitting on the sofa, rubbing her stomach, "Shit, I still can't believe what just happened. I need something to eat, but it's still some blood on the floor." Jada throws a pillow at her, "damn

Melissa, could you not think about stuffing your face. We are facing some off-the-wall shit right now." Melissa sucks her teeth, "My bad, sue me for being an emotional eater." Jada glanced at her brother, "I'm curious. Why aren't you upset, Daryl?"

He looks at his sister, laid back on the couch, glaring at him, "Because I know Daddy for who he is, he's a snake. I used to ask Daddy about Shanel; he would tell me she is an evil curse. I went to visit her on the job and didn't tell her who I was. She helped me put together my college portfolio. She was rather pleasant and had so many awards on her wall. I don't understand why our daddy called her an evil curse Jada."

Jada massages her head, "Well, Sharon is taking it hard because she trusted everything Daddy said. I did, too, until I read that letter Daddy wrote Shanel. My mama used to tell me you got to know the spirit by the spirit; I wish I listened to my spirit instead of my flesh. I would have cut Daddy out of my life a long time ago." Jada's cell phone rings: she takes her phone off her hip, and she said, "Sharon how are you?"

Sharon softly spoke, "Jada, my heart dropped to my stomach the entire time I was riding with Daddy to the hospital. The police asked me a million questions; I'm so drained, Jada."

The doorbell rings while she is talking to Sharon on the phone. Daryl goes to answer the door. The police walk into the den and begin talking to Melissa. Jada asked, "What did the doctor say about Daddy's condition?"

Sharon said, "Our daddy attempted suicide didn't go in his favor. He shot his ear off and grazed the side of his head. He did lose a lot of blood which caused him to go into a coma. The way he shot himself, the bullet didn't penetrate his brain, he shot upward."

Hold on, Sharon, "Excuse me Y'all, just a quick update on daddy; he's in a coma." Daryl shakes his head; Jada continues talking to Sharon, "Somebody needs to call Shanel and let her know what happened to Daddy." Said, Sharon

Jada replied, "Well, the police have returned to the house talking to Daryl and Melissa. I will call her after the police leave."

Sharon slowly breathes into the phone, "Okay, I'll keep y'all posted on daddy's condition," Jada hangs up with her sister focusing her attention on the conversation with the officer, Daryl, and her cousin Melissa. The officer walks into the kitchen with Melissa taking notes and pictures of the crime scene again. The officer asked a couple more questions and then walked out the front door. Jada joins her cousin in the kitchen, and she looks down at the blood on the floor with tears in her eyes. Melissa shakes her head in disbelief, "Man, when I woke up this morning, never in a million years would I have thought in my lifetime that I would witness some shit like this. This is crazy, How could Uncle Darren do this to himself? I don't understand people."

Jada continues looking at the blood on the floor, "We need to clean up this blood," Melissa shakes her head, "Nope, I wiped up as much blood as I could earlier." Jada frowns, "Heifer go find me some bleach." Daryl walks into the kitchen, "I'm glad that officer left, dang this a lot of blood to clean up," Melissa look underneath the kitchen sink, Daryl said, "We have all the cleaning products and rags in the utility closet." Melissa walks to the closet to grab the bucket and cleaning supplies. She fills the bucket with bleach and hot water to clean the floor. She said, "I'll mop up the blood,"

Jada said, "Well, somebody needs to call Shanel and tell her know what happened to Daddy."

Melissa frowns, "I'm not calling her,"

Daryl glares at Melissa, "I'll do it; as a matter of fact, I'll finish cleaning up Daddy's blood. Y'all go home and change out those bloody clothes. You still need to meet Sharon at the hospital." Jada sighs, "Are you sure, Lil bro," Daryl nods. Jada walked into the den, where Sharon threw her purse and keys. "All right, Melissa, let's go," she grabbed her coach bag, "I'm right behind you, Jada," The neighbors were still outside trying to ask Jada and Melissa questions as they walked to the car. Daryl walks outside, talking to one of the neighbors about the ordeal that happened to their daddy. Melissa and Jada drove off listening to Babyface.

Daryl walks back into the house to the kitchen, cleaning up the blood on the floor and wall with bleach. He dumps the water outside the back door. He walks upstairs to shower quickly, getting his daddy's life off his body. Daryl got out of the shower, quickly dried off, and got dressed. He went downstairs to look for his daddy's cell phone. He went through his daddy's contacts and found Shanel's number, and he nervously pushed her name; it dialed twice before she picked up, "Hello."

Daryl's lips tremble, "may I speak to Shanel?"

She politely asked, "Who is this?"

Daryl hesitated before speaking, "I'm Darren's son, Daryl,"

"Shanel sighed, "What can I do for you?"

he stutters, "Uh, uh, uh, h-h-how c-c-can I put it?"

Shanel became annoyed, "Just say it,"

Daryl quickly spits the words out, "Daddy shot himself."

"That a sad situation. Is he dead?" asked Shanel.

Daryl replied, "No, he is in a coma, Daddy shot his ear off and grazed the side of his head." Sharon rode in the ambulance with him to the hospital. Jada and Melissa went home to change before going out to the hospital."

Shanel asked, "So y'all were there when the donor you call daddy shot himself."

Daryl chuckles, "Yes, why do you call Dad, the donor?" She said, "Because he was never a father to me, he just donated his sperm."

"Wow, you cut a throat kind of woman. I like it, sis,"

Shanel said, "Yeah, it comes from dealing with shady family members. Well, I need to go, uh…"

He chuckles, "Daryl."

"Just keep me posted, I guess," said Shanel.

Okay."

Chapter 11

I can't believe the donor they call dad, son just called me. I need to call Damon about this. I call his cell phone he answers on the second ring, "What's up?"

"Any news on your cousin Dee?"

"Yeah, he was killed in your neighborhood this morning." My heart hit the floor, "Oh my lord, that happened across the street from Ms. Waters' house this morning. Damn it is too much crap going on today."

"What else happened today?" Asked Damon

"Well, the donor they call dad son Daryl called to tell me that Darren shot his ear off and grazed the side of his head."

"What the hell!? Are you going to see about him?"

"No, Damon, I don't wanna be bothered with my sisters putting me down. I cannot take another rejection from the donor they call dad in person in front of my sisters. I sigh, enough of my family drama, so what happened to your cousin?"

Damon sighed, "Well, from what the girl said, Dee messed over her a while back. When she saw him in the club, she seduced him back to her place to settle the score."

"Dang, Dee must have really hurt that woman."

"Shanel, I just told my cousin a week before he got killed, that karma was going bite him in the ass; I just didn't think it was going to result in death."

I shake my head, "You already know the wages of sin is death. Hold on, I have a call on the other line, hello,"

"Shanel, this Jada," I cut her off before she could finish her sentence. "I already know, Daryl called me." "Well, are you coming to the hospital?" asked Jada.

I said, "No, he has his daughters with him. Besides, he does not need the child he called a curse to show up while he is recovering. He might just die."

"Shanel, please, be the bigger person and support Daddy." Said Jada

"My answer is no, goodbye," I click back on the line with Damon, "I'm back; that was Jada,"

Damon said, "You need to go see your daddy,"

I sigh, "I'm not going to the hospital,"

Damon said, "I'll go with you, Shanel."

I asked, "What about Josh?"

"He can come, I'll stay in the waiting room with Josh," said Damon. I sigh, "I don't know, the donor does not like me." "I am not going to force you; it's your decision Shanel." said Damon.

"Hold on Damon," he said, "I'm on my way home,"

"Okay, I'll see you in a little bit."

I answer the other line, "Hello."

"Shanel…" I interrupted my mom before she could finish, "I already know what happened."

"What are you talking about, Shanel?"

I replied, "Darren shot himself."

My mother screamed, "What the hell!? Oh, my goodness! Did you have anything to do with this Shanel?"

I replied, "No, why would you say that mama?"

"You probably cursed your daddy to shoot himself," said Ms. Howard

"You sound really ignorant, mother," Ms. Howard laughs, "Your daddy said you are a curse to the family. Why aren't you home?" I said, "ugh! Mother, you are evil. It is none of your business if I come home or not,"

Ms. Howard replied, "It is my business. I am worried about my grandson. I am parked out in front of your townhouse waiting on you for an hour."

I said, "I'll get there when I get there,"

"You're so damn rude; I'm getting tired of your attitude Shanel,"

I said, "Then stop calling and leave me alone mother. I need to put a restraining order on you first thing in the morning."

"For what? I am your damn mother," I hung up the phone, the nerve of my mother. Damon walks through the front door. "Shanel,"

I replied, "I am sitting in the living room on the sofa."

Damon walks in and flops on the loveseat across from me, "Man, my family is in an uproar about who's going to help pay for Dee's funeral services; I can't deal with my family right now."

I frown, "Dee didn't have an insurance policy,"

"Hell no, you know they will make me foot the bill." Said Damon

I frown, "No, the family should come together and help out." Damon said, "Shanel we are talking about my always crying broke family,"

I sighed, shaking my head, "Well, they shouldn't put all the responsibility on you," Damon rubbed his head, "Anymore word on your dad's condition,"

"I sigh, looking up to the heavens, "No, and I don't really care, Damon."

"Shanel let me school you on this situation; I know your daddy has put you through so much hurt and pain. You need to forgive him so God can truly bless you. How can you ask God to forgive you for all your sins, and you cannot forgive your daddy?"

I glare at Damon, "Do not give me that look; you know I'm right, Shanel. The key word for today is "forgiveness." Now, can you do that for God?" I throw a pillow at him, "You're right, Damon?"

"I know, Ms. Waters beat the bible upside my head; I mean literally, she hit me upside head with the bible. That woman doesn't play about her bible." I burst out laughing rolling off the sofa to the floor "That's not funny," said Damon.

I said, "Whatever, that's what you get,"

"So, what you going to do about your daddy?" I shrug my shoulders, "Shanel, don't let time pass you by," I get up from the floor, "I hear you, Damon,"

He asked, "Where is Josh?"

"He's upstairs enjoying his room."

"I'm going to check on my boy," I sat on the sofa thinking about what Damon said, "Lord, I need your help on this one." I get up from the sofa and walk upstairs to my room to pray about the situation.

96

Chapter 12

Jada and Melissa finally made it to the hospital. They saw Sharon standing outside their daddy's room talking to his wife. She still had on her bloody clothes. "Hey Deborah, how are you holding up?"

She frowns, "I am angry at your father for being so stupid. Did anybody see my son Daryl?"

Jada replied, "No, we're just getting here," Deborah pulls her cell phone out of her purse, "Can you excuse me? I need to call Daryl."

"Sure, go ahead," said Sharon. Deborah walks away, dialing her son's number.

Sharon asked, "Did anybody get a hold of Shanel?"

Jada frowns, "Yeah, I called and told her what happened to Dad. She is not coming. I wouldn't blame her after all the hell we put her through. I despise myself for the things I said to her." "How do you think I feel?" Said, Sharon

"I bought you some clothes." Said Jada

"I cannot believe Uncle Darren did that to Shanel. I mean, using voodoo to keep her down, that is just evil." said Melissa.

Sharon shakes her head and disgust, "I thought voodoo was a myth."

"No, I heard many people say that it won't affect you if you don't believe in it." Said, Melissa

Jada shakes her head in disagreement, "That is not true. It talks about sorcery and witchcraft in the Bible; churches just push it under the rug. Hell, church folks dabble in voodoo. We know firsthand; look at our daddy."

"Oh, my goodness Jada, Daddy is a deacon in the church. It is true what the Bible says. Everybody says, lord, lord will not enter the kingdom of heaven. Daddy portrays himself as a righteous man who dedicated his life to the word of God." Said a hurtful Sharon.

Jada frowns, "he was straddling the fence trying to serve two masters, which the devil almost won."

Sharon agrees, "Yeah, you get hurt Straddling the fence," Melissa taps Sharon, "Is that Shanel's mother coming this way? Why is she dressed like she going to the club?"

Sharon sighs heavily, "Oh Lord, that's all we need. Why is she here? Daddy hasn't talked to her in years.

"Hey, where is Darren? Never mind, move out my way, tramps. I see his wife," said Ms. Howard

"Lord, she's lucky my mama raised me to respect my elders; let's get a snack before I beat that heifer down." Said Jada.

Sharon said, "I need to change my clothes, can y'all bring me back a candy bar?" Ms. Howard interrupts Deborah's phone conversation, "What can I do for you, Shelley?"

"I need to see Darren right now." Deborah points to his room, Ms. Howard walks into his room, smirking. "You better wake your trifling ass up, you dumb fuck. Why in the hell did you shoot yourself?" Shanel walks in on her mother, "You shoulda shot Shanel instead; that girl is evil, a failure, and a waste of life. You were supposed to kill her ass, not yourself, bastard." I run out of Darren's room with tears running down my face; she shouts at Damon, "I knew I should not have come here!" I run to the elevator, "You stay here, Josh, let me go check on your mama," Damon runs after Shanel, "Jada, stop Shanel before she gets on the elevator." I broke away from my sister, got on the elevator, and quickly closed the door. Melissa and Jada are looking confused, "What happened, Damon?" He sighs, "I do not know; just watch Josh for me, please. I need to find out what happened to Shanel."

"Okay," said Jada,

Sharon walks toward Melissa and Jada looking perplex "what's going on?" Melissa and Jada shrug their shoulders, Sharon said "Daddy must be up," they rushed back to their daddy's room and busted in on Shanel's mother talking to their father. Sharon shouts, "What the hell did you do to Shanel this time?"

Ms. Howard frowns, "Shanel was not in here."

"She had to be," said Jada.

"Look, tramps, I have been alone talking to Darren. Shanel did not come in here. Now leave me the hell alone." Said Ms. Howard,

An older nurse walks into Daddy's room with Deborah, "Ladies keep your voices down, or I am going to have security remove you from the hospital. Do I make myself clear?" Nobody said anything; the nurse walked out, mumbling under her breath. Deborah cuts her eyes at Ms. Howard; she walks out of her husband's room. Jada approaches Ms. Howard, "You need to leave right now."

She chuckles, "I have every right to be here just like you. Darren and I have a daughter together. Now you can get the hell out, so I can spend time with Darren."

"You are a trifling ass woman with no class. You are not even married to my daddy, Deborah is, now show her some respect." Said Jada,

Ms. Howard smirks, "How's your mother, Jada?" Sharon and Melissa had to grab Jada from whooping Ms. Howard ass. "Let's go, Jada, don't waste your time on that bitch," said Melissa,

Sharon glances at her nephew, "Hey Josh, how are you, sweetie?"

He smiles, "I'm doing good auntie."

Sharon asked, "Melissa, can you watch Josh while I talk to Jada alone."

"Sure," Sharon takes Jada by the hand and walks her into the bathroom. "Girl why are you letting Ms. Howard get underneath your skin; you know she's the devil."

She replied, "I know, you know how I feel about my mom."

"I understand, but do not let that nasty slimy ass Ms. Howard know how much that bothers you. Hell, we need to figure out what happened in Daddy's room to make Shanel storm out the way she did."

Jada wipes the tears out of her eyes, "It ain't no telling with those two; I can't trust Daddy no more,"

"Hell, nobody can; I feel sorry for his wife and son. Where did Deborah go anyway?" Asked Sharon

Jada replied, "She walked in the room with the nurse, then disappeared after that." Jada wiped her face, "I hope she okay, having to deal with Ms. Howard's trifling ass." They left the bathroom and sat by Melissa and their nephew Josh.

Melissa asked, "Are you okay, Jada?"

"Yeah, is Ms. Howard still in the room with my daddy?" Melissa nods,

Jada frowns, "I wish her ass just leave," Sharon nods in agreement, "Ms. Howard keep conflict in the family. What did Daddy see in her anyway?"

Sharon shakes her head, "I don't know, sis." She looks at her nephew, rubbing his tummy.

"Are you hungry, Josh?"

He replied, "No, ma'am." Sharon and Jada sat silently, waiting for their daddy to wake up. Meanwhile, Damon finally caught up with Shanel outside the hospital, about to walk toward the parking garage. "Shanel, stop running, Shanel, stop!"

I asked, "What do you want, Damon?"

He asked, "What the hell happened in the room with your dad?"

"It was my mama, the things that she said about me; they were trying to kill me," I began crying like a baby. Damon hugged me, "I am so sorry." A young, slender, brown-skinned, well-manicured gentleman with a low cut wearing a polo shirt, black jeans, and black Nikes walks up, "Is this Shanel?"

Damon sized him up, "Who the hell are you?"

"I'm sorry, my name is Daryl; Shanel is my sister."

"My bad," said Damon.

I lifted my head off Damon's chest; he said, "Your brother Daryl is here to meet you." I wipe my eyes away.

I looked puzzled. "Hold up, you look familiar. I cannot place your face right now," Daryl smiles, showing his off-white teeth. "I came to your job a couple of days ago," My eyes grew large, "Yes, you did; why didn't you say anything?"

Daryl replied, "I was nervous you might recognize me from a year ago. You helped me put my portfolio together for college."

I frowned, "So I'm assuming you went to the college of your choice." Daryl chuckles, "I went to the college of Daddy's choice." Daryl's mother comes outside, "There you go, where have you been,"
"I am just getting here, mom. Have you met Daddy's other daughters, Shanel?" Daryl's mom had a surprised look on her face. "No, I have not; your dad never mentioned her to me." Daryl frowns, shaking his head. "It figures,"

I smiled, "I'm Shelley Howard's daughter." Daryl's mom extends her hand to me, "I'm Deborah, your father's wife; nice to meet you," I happily shake her hand, "Likewise, and this is my son's dad, Damon," Deborah shakes his hand, she begins to chuckle, "So Shelly is your mother, I would have never known. "This family has too many dang secrets," Daryl glanced at me, then back at his mother, "Well, I am going to go inside the hospital. I will be in the waiting room with your other sisters," said Mrs. Deborah,"

Daryl replied, "Okay, Mom, I'll be up shortly," I frowned at Daryl, "Why did you lie about who you were when you came to my office,"

He replied, "I was scared you were going to make me leave or call the police." Damon chuckled; I cut my eyes at him, and Shanel asked, "Why would I do that?"

Daryl replied, "I didn't know how you would feel about daddy son coming to see you,"

Shanel glared at Daryl, "In spite of what you heard about me, I'm not the mean sister with an attitude; I'm the hurt sister that has been rejected by my family,"

Daryl held his head down in shame, "I know that now, and I am sorry. I just wanted to get to know my sister. When I was fifteen, you called Daddy for help with graduation. He was saying hurtful, ill-mannered things to you. I could not understand why Daddy was so nasty to you. I used to eavesdrop on all daddy conversation." I held my hand up to Daryl, "Uh, can we not talk about the donor you call daddy," Daryl laughed, I'm sorry, sis, but I like the name you got for daddy." I frowned, glaring at my brother.

Daryl's laughter fades, "Sis, I would love to develop a relationship with you; I don't believe everything I hear. I get to know a person first before I pass judgment."

Shanel smiled, "Thou shall not judge Daryl; that's what the bible says."

"Sis, who actually follows the good book? Can you find me one person that follows the bible one hundred percent. I will give you mad props, sis." Damon chuckles, "that's going to be hard." I laugh, "You cool with me, lil bro." Daryl smiles, giving me a huge hug. "We need to go back inside I left poor Josh with your crazy sisters," said Damon, they rush back inside the hospital.

Chapter 13

Ms. Howard exits of out Darren's room, smiling Sharon and Jada. "I am finished, girls; your daddy is all yours now." Sharon sucks her teeth, "Get out my face Ms. Howard," I see my mother talking to my sisters. I ran up to my mother, pushing my sisters out the way. "Shanel, get out of my face."

I shout, "No!" My mother shoves me to the side. I run up to my mom, pushing her into the wall.

Ms. Howard screams, "You crazy bitch! Have you lost your damn mind?" The nurse warned them to keep quiet; I glared at my mother. "No, you and the donor they call daddy are crazy. You all hate me so much that you two plotted to kill me?" Sharon and Jada stand up, trying to calm me down, "Will you two stop crowding my space, Damn!" I focus my attention back to my mother. "How could a mother want to kill her daughter? I have a son; you are a selfish, evil woman with no compassion."

Ms. Howard cries, "You such a liar Shanel," Daryl walks up to Ms. Howard, "No, she not; before you all came over today, I eavesdropped on Daddy and Ms. Howard's phone conversation upstairs in my room. To be honest, it was more of Ms. Howard leaning toward the idea to kill you. Daddy was not keen on the idea at all." Ms. Howard chuckles, "Shanel baby, do you actually believe this tutti frutti?" Mrs. Deborah frowns, "Who in the hell are you calling tutti frutti? You slutty tramp, you need to leave right now,"

Ms. Howard smirks, "I will leave when I am good and ready. Shanel, I am your mother, I would not try and kill you,"

I said, "Mother, get out of my face."

"Shanel, don't you disrespect…" I slapped my mother in the face; she flew to the floor, and everybody was in shock. "Now I know what I heard in the donor they call daddy room. I am not stupid, Mother." Ms. Howard struggles to get up from the floor, "Do not blame me for your troubles. Your daddy started all this a long time ago, not me. I wanted you as a baby; your daddy disowned you. You need to be slapping him."

I look at my mother with so much pain in my eyes, "You are a liar, Mother. Damon, let's go, and where is my son?"

"He's with Melissa in the other waiting room," said Jada.

"Go get our child so we can go," Damon goes to the waiting room to get Josh.

"Shanel, can we talk," I gave Jada a straight attitude, "Jada, get the hell out of my face. I am not in the mood right now."

"Shanel, please, will you talk to me?" she walks away from Jada, shaking her head. Damon walks past everybody with his son. Jada calls Damon, he turns toward her, "Can you tell Shanel I'm sorry and for her to give me a call,"

He sighs, rubbing his head, "Okay, but do you think she wants to talk to you all right now? Give her some time; she has a lot of shit to process." Damon sighs and shakes his head, "I gotta go," Damon rushes to catch up with Shanel; she is already sitting in the car waiting for Damon and Josh. He buckles Josh in the backseat, then gets in the car, "are you okay, Shanel?" I turn to him with hurt in my eyes, "I can't believe this night; I should have never gone to the hospital," He cranks up his BMW car and drives. "Shanel, whether you like it or not, going to the hospital help open up your eyes about your family."

"I guess, but my mother feels she doesn't do anything wrong. She makes me sick; I cannot stand her ass. She is always addressing everybody's faults, just like her mother. She smothered her children. Even when they were in their 30s, she continued to treat them like children. That is why the family went their separate ways. Hell, I have not seen my two aunties and uncles since I was ten. I do not remember them returning to my grandmother's funeral either."

"Damn, that's just sad. It sounds like your mom does not know how to be an adult because your grandma would not let them grow up and live." Said Damon.

I stared out the window, looking up at the stars. "I could remember my mother would tell me how she would save money to get out on her own. Somehow, my grandmother would catch wind of what she was doing. She would make her hand over her money so my mother wouldn't move out. See, my grandmother was getting a disability check, which was little to nothing, so she would take from her kids to maintain her so-call keeping up with the Jones' lifestyle."

Damon chuckles, "Those Joneses will keep your ass in debt, trying to live a life you can't afford."

I frown, "But to hear my grandmother tell it, she doesn't recall any of that happening."

"That is called denial. Did you have a close relationship with your grandmother?" asked Damon.

I rub my temples, "Nope, she called me a sinner baby because I was born out of wedlock; she would not hold me or acknowledge me as her grandchild. My auntie told me that my so-called Holy Bible-reading grandmother would call me Satan baby. I begin to cry; I was born into an evil family."

"Well, you don't have to worry about the past anymore. I am here for you," said Damon.

I sigh wiping my tears, "I cannot forget about the past when it is still affecting my present life. Hello, look what is going on around me now."

Damon glances at me and keeps his eye on the road simultaneously, "I understand, but you can't give negative energy charge over your life when God is showing you that within a storm, he's still blessing you."

I sigh rubbing my curly ponytail, "I hear what you are saying, but how can you enjoy your blessing when your mother and the donor they call dad are trying to do me off,"

Damon hit the driving wheel; I flinched; he said, "Oh my goodness, after all the hell you have been through, you still can't see how God has kept you through all your trial and tribulation. You need to stop complaining so damn much and start praising God for not letting your mother and daddy plot against you take place. Just be happy. God allowed you to live another day to spend time with your son." I lean over to kiss Damon on the cheek, "You're right, Damon,"

"Girl, I know you too well. You say I'm right, but you'll go back into that complaining mode again, and you really need to trust that God is working everything out for your good. You must forgive your family to move forward with your life."

I look at Damon, "What has gotten into you? I mean, I have never heard you talk like this before,"

"Damon laughs as he pulls up in the driveway, cutting off the engine, "Ms. Waters and her bible; I told you that woman beat me down with the bible while smoking her weed." We get out of the car laughing, "I'll get the sleepy head out the backseat," said Damon; I open the front door cutting on all the lights in the house; Damon comes in behind me with our son knocked out in his arms, "No roaches," he chuckles. I walk over to Damon to Josh kiss on the forehead. "I'm going to put him in bed." I smile, looking around at the blessing that God has given me, "I'm sorry God, you have been listening to my cries, I have been selfish," Damon comes downstairs, "Yes you have, but God forgives you, now what?"

"Well, I am going to bed. Goodnight," Damon frowned. "Can you bring me a blanket?"

I stopped midway in my steps turning to Damon, "Why don't you sleep in your son's room? He has an extra bed," Damon mumbles, "I would rather cuddle with you,"

I asked, "You said something?"

Damon frowned, "Nah, I'm going upstairs with Josh," I continued walking upstairs to my bedroom and closed the door. Damon sat on the sofa, "Man, it's getting hard to control my feelings for Shanel; they are getting stronger every day." Damon walks upstairs, "I need to take an ice-cold shower."

Chapter 14

Sharon and Jada are sitting in the room with their daddy. Daryl walks in with coffee, "Here, I thought you all might need some caffeine to ease your nerves; this has been a very hectic day. I am going to call it a night,"

"All right," said Sharon.

How is your mother holding up?" asked Jada.

He chuckles, "Let's see, her husband is a fucken devil; I'm just glad she can't sweep this under the rug anymore. She must face the situation at hand." he hugged his sisters, "Goodnight," Melissa walked into the room; Daryl hugged her on his way out the room, "Are you all leaving anytime soon? I do have to go to work in the morning."

"You can take the car," said Jada; she picked up her coach bag from the floor, looking for the keys, "Here you go," Melissa yawned, "Thanks, I'll call you tomorrow," Sharon and Jada looked at each other with tired eyes, "We need to do smoothing. We cannot continue to let this confusion corrupt our family life." Said, Sharon

Jada taps Sharon with excitement, "Why don't we get Pastor Dobbin to help," Sharon agrees, "Yeah, before somebody gets killed," Jada smiles, "I'll call him first thing tomorrow morning."

Sharon pauses, looking at her sister. "Hold up, we have a problem. How are we going to get everybody to come in for counseling at the same time? That is going to be a big challenge, Jada."

Jada smiled, "Ole ye of little faith, you got to believe Sista like Peter and don't doubt like Thomas," Sharon kissed her sister on the forehead, "I just realized we are stuck at the damn hospital; I need to call Melissa." said Jada, she uses the phone in her dad room, "hey Melissa did you leave out the parking lot yet?"

She said, "No, I realize that Sharon rode in the ambulance, and we drove her car to your place."

Jada smiled, "well I'm coming down," Sharon frowns, "I'm not staying here by myself with Daddy,"

Jada chuckles, "Well, you better come on, Sista girl."

Sharon heavily sighs, "Let me have a minute with Daddy,"

"Okay, sis," Jada walks out of her daddy's room. Sharon stares at her daddy in disgust, gets up from her chair, walks over to her daddy's lifeless body, and slaps him in the face, "Wake up, you coward. I am praying that the heavenly Father will wake up from this coma, so you can face all your transgressions. You are a bastard, and to think I worship the ground you walked on. Your life has been one big lie; how could you hurt Shanel like that? I do not get you, Daddy; you had Jada and me thinking that Shanel was this awful person. You were the devil in our life all this time, leading us down the road of destruction, you! you! You always quote bible verses telling Jada and me to repent when we did something wrong in your eyes. Did you repent, Daddy, before you shot yourself? Answer me!" Sharon grabs her daddy, shaking him, "Answer me! I hate you! I hate you!" the nurse comes in the room and grabs Sharon, "Ma'am, you need to leave, or I will have the hospital security escort you out."

"Get off me!" said Sharon. Two other nurses came into the room to see what all the commotion was about. Sharon glances at her dad and then looks at the nurse, "You do whatever it takes to wake his ass up out of this coma," Sharon walks to the chair to get her coach bag staggering out of her daddy's room. She gets on the elevator, crying, clutching her bag close to her chest. "Lord, why did I have to have a daddy like Darren? Why lord? Why lord? I hate him so much, lord." Sharon gets off the elevator, wiping her face. Jada parked in front of the entrance, Sharon gets in the car. "You good sis,"

"No, I need to call my man so he can hold me tonight in my time of need, she looks in her coach bag for her cell phone while Jada drives. She calls her man; he picks up on the three-ring. Sharon puts him on speaker, "Hey baby, can I come over tonight? I had a bad night; I need you to destress me, if you know what I mean," Melissa and Jada chuckle,

"Nah, you can't come over; I have company." Sharon takes the phone off the speaker.

"What? You better get rid of that broad," said Sharon.

He replied, "Look, we can't see each other anymore. My broad is pregnant with twins, but we can still have our fuck session if you want."

"You a sorry ass, I don't know what I ever saw in you?" "My big dick," Sharon ends her call, "I can't believe his ass,"

"Sharon, you know that man was still kicking it with his ex-girlfriend. You thought that because you have money, he would leave her? He was manipulating you to stay and take care of both of them. Hell, I saw that a mile away." said Melissa.

Sharon replied in a spicy tone, "I didn't ask you for your damn two cents,"

"And I didn't ask for a dumb cousin." Said, Melissa

Sharon frowns, "bitch, you must wanna walk home,"

"Hey, stop it, you two. We do not need any more added drama to the equation." Said Jada. They drove in silently, listening to Ralph Tresvant's Sensitivity, until Sharon began singing along with him. Jada asked, "who sang that song?"

Sharon replied, "Duh, sexy ass Ralph Tresvant?"

"Then let him sing it," Sharon and Melissa chuckle, "shut up heifer, I can sing,"

Jada chuckles, "Keep telling yourself that, sis," Jada pulls up to Melissa's apartments, "I see you shining girl. These are nice, Melissa. I am glad you finally moved out on your own." Sharon frowned, "You say this every time we come over here."

"Thanks, girl; I'll see y'all later,"

Jada smiled, "All right Melissa," she glanced at her sis, shaking her head. "Sis, you need to fix your face."

Sharon frowned, "She makes me sick,"

"You just mad because she read your ass; the truth hurt, sis,"

"Whatever, Jada, why are we still here?"

Jada replied, "I am making sure she gets into her apartment safely. Girl, calm your ass down," Melissa waved to let them know she was good. Jada pulls out of the parking lot, "I'm going home with you; I'm too upset to be by myself," said Sharon.

Jada said, "I'm sorry, sis, but I need my quiet time, if you know what I mean,"

She looked confused, "you don't even have a man, heifer."

Jada said, "You do not need a man to have fun. I have plenty batteries,"

Sharon glared at her, "Our daddy could be on his deathbed, and you worry about getting an orgasm,"

"Hold up, Ms. I can't be alone tonight, don't get mad at me because your so call man dissed your ass tonight."

Sharon said, "You must wanna walk home, heifer,"

She replied, "You must've forgotten who's driving the car,"

Sharon cut her eyes, "You are working my last nerves, Jada," She smirks at her sister, "Then take your ass home."

"Damn, Jada, you are kicking me to the curve for a dildo?"

She has a huge smile, "Yes, I am," Jada pulls up to her townhome, putting the car in park. She gets out of the car without saying a word to her sister. Sharon slides over to the driver seat, mumbling. "Ole crazy heifer." Then drives off,

Chapter 15

Jada's alarm clock wakes her up; she looks at the clock, throws her pillow, and knocks the alarm clock to the floor; the alarm is still going off. "Lord, why does morning come so quick?" she gets out of the bed, scratching her head. I do not feel like going to work dealing with people's nasty attitudes. Why the hell couldn't I have been born into a rich ass family? Goodness, I am tired of working. Lord, can you send me a good man with money?" Jada walks into the bathroom, looking at herself in the mirror, "I hate that I look like Darren," she puts her hair in a ponytail, turns on the stereo, listens to Ralph Tresvant's Sensitivity, "I do need a Man with Sensitivity," Jada walks into the bathroom to take a shower, her phone rings, "Why is it every time I'm taking a shower, or on the toilet, people wanna call, Damn!" she wraps a towel around her body to check her cell phone, "I'll call you back Sharon," Sharon walks in Jada room, "whatever, why are you not answering your phone?" Jada glared at her sister, "My bad, you have company?"

Jada replied, "Uh, no, I was trying to take a shower. Why are you over here so damn early in the morning?"

Sharon flops on Jada's bed, "I could not sleep; my brain will not turn the hell off. It keeps rewinding to yesterday. Jada, I am stressed the hell out."

"I hear you, sis, but I need to finish taking a shower." Said Jada,

Sharon frowns, "Hurry up. I want to get breakfast." Jada takes a quick shower and comes out of the bathroom in her bra and panties in ten minutes. "Did you have time to call the pastor yet?" Jada reaches for her housecoat in the closet, "Uh, no, I will call him before I leave. I am not due in the office until ten this morning."

"Shoot, I was hoping to carpool with you this morning; oh well I am about to leave. Let me know what Pastor Dobbins says," said Sharon.

"All right, sis," as soon as Jada heard the front door close, she reached for her cell phone on the nightstand and began dialing the Pastor's number. He answered, "This is the day that the lord has made, let us rejoice in Jesus' name. This is Pastor Dobbins, how can I help you today?"

"Praise the lord, Pastor Dobbins, this Jada Spivey."

"Good morning, Jada. What can I do for you on this blessed day?"

"Well, Pastor Dobbins, it's too much drama going on with my family."

He said, "Jada, all family have problems,"

"Yeah, that's true, but my family is busted up and disgusted with each other," he sighs, "what's going on, Jada?"

"My daddy shot himself,"

"Oh, my lord, what caused him to do something like that?" asked Pastor Dobbins,

Jada replied, "All I can say is my daddy's double lifestyle has caught up with him." He sighs heavily, "I can't believe what I'm hearing; if there's anything I can do, just let me know." Jada smiles, "Well, there is, I want to get all my family together, so you can help us deal with this situation, and not continue to cover it up with a band-aid."

"I'll try my best, Jada, to help your family," Jada gets excited, "Thank you Pastor Dobbins, "I'll email all their contact information."

He asked, "When do you want to have this family meeting?"

Jada said, "The sooner, the better, Pastor Dobbins,"

"Okay, I'll get on it right away, Jada,"

"Thanks, Pastor Dobbins,"

He said, "You be blessed, Jada," she hung up the phone, "Lord, I hope my family can heal and move forward." Jada begins to get ready for work, and her cell phone rings, "dammit, it never fails, hello!" "Why are you so damn loud? You are about to blow my eardrum out," said Sharon.

"I'm trying to get ready for work; what do you want?"

Sharon replied, "Ms. Attitude, I wanted to know if you had a chance to call Pastor Dobbins?"

"Yes, I did, and he agreed to meet with the family,"

"Well, did you tell him about Daddy," asked Sharon. She answered in a frustrated tone, "Yes, Sharon, he was in shock. Now I need to go so I can finish getting ready for work. I have a busy day ahead of me. Talk to you later." Jada hangs up with her sister looking at the time, "Damn, I am going to be late. I will be doing eighty on 400; thank goodness they got rid of the toll booths.

Sharon is still looking at the phone, "I know that heifer didn't just rush my ass off the phone," Sharon calls the hospital to get an update on her daddy. The nurse lets her know he is still in a coma. She hangs up the phone with the nurse, "Daddy, the lord is not going to let you get off that easy. You will have to face your demons," Sharon sits back in her chair at work, sipping on her coffee.

Chapter 16

Damon walks into the townhome. "Hey, Shanel. Where are you?" I replied, "I'm upstairs,"

He asked, "Are you dressed?"

"Yes," he slightly runs upstairs to my room, "where is Josh?"

I smile, sitting on my bed, "I took him to the learning center at the clubhouse,"

"Was he excited?" asked Damon.

I replied, "Beyond excitement, he was rushing out the door." Damon sat in the chair next to my dresser, "I just came by to check on you this afternoon; I ended up leaving last night to go to a hotel. Don't ask any questions. I am about to go and take care of your old townhouse; a couple of friends are coming to help me. You did take all your important documents out of the townhome?"

"Yes, bighead," my cell phone rings. I get up from my bed, walk to my big boy reaching for the phone, "Hello,"

"Hello Shanel, this is Pastor Dobbins," I look at Damon with a puzzled look, "How are you, Pastor?"

He answers, "I am blessed, in Jesus. I was wondering if you could come by the church tomorrow so we can talk?" I fidget with my hair, "Uh, about what, Pastor Dobbins?"

He said, "Well, Jada called me…" Shanel sighed heavily, "Pastor, let me stop you now. I do not want to talk about my dysfunctional family."

"Shanel, your family should come to the church for counseling. You all can resolve these deep-rooted issues that have been plaguing your family for years. Now, you can continue to let it affect your future or address the situation and find a solution."

"I hear what you are saying, Pastor Dobbins. I am not sure that would be a good idea right now, due to the current event that has occurred in my family."

"Shanel, I am not going to beg, no grown person. You are either going to participate in the counseling or not." Said Pastor Dobbins

I replied, "It's not that easy, Pastor Dobbins,"

He asked, "Do you have faith in God, Shanel?" I stutter, "I-I-I-do, but I have been through so much."

He said, "So did Jesus. What is your point, Shanel? You need to stop starting, directing, and producing your pity party. Now get it together, young lady."

I heavily sigh through the phone, "Can I call you back, pastor Dobbins?"

"Sure, don't tarry on this, Shanel." Said Dobbins

"Yes, sir," I hang up the phone; Damon looks at me, "Who was that?"

I said, "Pastor Dobbins, apparently, Jada called him about our dysfunctional family. He wants to meet with the family to help us with our deep-rooted issues, that has been plaguing our family for years." Damon smiles, "I think you should participate. Maybe Pastor Dobbins can help you, Shanel." I frown, "Pastor Dobbins doesn't know what he's getting himself into. My family is evil as hell," Damon chuckles, "Well, I hope Jada warned him." I nod in agreement, "Call him back and let him know that you will participate in the family counseling." I sigh, "I will," Damon begins walking downstairs to the front door, "I need to go meet with these people," I walked behind him and asked, "When are you leaving to go back to California?"

Damon opens the front door, "After my cousin's funeral, what are your plans today?"

I smile, "Well, I think I'm going to finish working on Josh's baby scrapbook, it soothes my nerves."

"Well, knock yourself out; I'll be back later today, so I can take you shopping for new clothes and shoes." Said Damion

I look around my townhome smiling; I go upstairs to my bedroom and sit on the edge of the bed, talking to God.

"Father God, in the name of Jesus, I do not understand your purpose for me. I have been struggling with my family constantly putting me down all my life. My life has been one big roller coaster ride; I want it to stop so I can get off. One minute Damon and I were fussing with one another. Now, he wants to do right by me and his son after talking to his friend and Ms. Waters. I should be happy that things are going well for Josh and me, but I cannot. I don't know how long this happiness is going to last before the devil tries and destroy my life again. Hell, I have the hardest time trusting people due to my family's evil Mishap. My family track record isn't the best. My mother and the donor they call daddy plotted to try and kill me. Then the donor they call daddy shot himself. How do I find peace in my life when things around me are falling apart, God? How do I trust people again, God? I have been down this road so many times. Help me to understand your purpose for me, God." I finish my talk with God. I look at myself in the mirror, "I have so much baggage in my life that I'm starting to age ungracefully." I sigh as I get up from the bed, looking in my closet for the big black trash bag of important papers. "Ahh found it," I pull the bag out the closet and drags it downstairs, "man this bag is heavy," I lift the trash bag on the table. "Dang, I almost broke my back." I sat down at the kitchen table, going through my bag and sorting out Josh's baby pictures. "My baby was so chunky and cute." I continued smiling and sorting all the different clippings I had kept over the years. I paused for a second and reached for my cell phone to call Pastor Dobbins back, "Hello, Pastor Dobbins, this is Shanel,"

He asked, "Have you decided on the family counseling?"

I replied, "I'll participate, Pastor Dobbins,"

He said, "You made the right decision, Shanel,"

I asked, "So when is this counseling thing?" Pastor Dobbins' tone became firm, "It is not a counseling thing, Shanel. I need you to come with an open mind, and it is tomorrow at ten a.m."

I frown, "That's short notice, Pastor Dobbins,"

He replied, "I know, but your sisters took that day off, and Melissa was already off. Your mother will also be attending."

I angrily asked, "My mother, why is she coming?"

Pastor Dobbins replied, "Shanel, the door is open for your family to heal. Remember, God is merciful, loving, and forgiving. Let me ask you this question: Shanel, how can you ask Jesus for forgiveness when you can't forgive your own family?"

I sigh, "I'm working on that, Pastor."

He said, "Well, you are not trying hard enough. You need to knock that wall down that is keeping you from forgiving your family."

I replied, "Pastor Dobbins, it is not that easy. I cannot forgive my family overnight. It does not work like that, not in the real world anyway."

He chuckles, "Shanel, if you have that mustard seed of faith, you can. You can move mountains, walk on water, and knock down your walls of obstacles. God is bigger than any problem you have in your life. Shanel, see this as a new beginning, no more secrets, hurt, or pain."

"I hear what you are saying, Pastor Dobbins. I guess, I will see you tomorrow." I hang up with the Pastor and continue working on my son's scrapbook. My cell phone rings, I glance at my phone smiling, reaching to pick it up, "Hey, Ms. Waters, how are you?"

She said, "I'm feeling good as ever; I just took my feel-good medicine, if you know what I mean."

I laugh, "Yes, I do,"

She asked, "Are you happy?"

I smile, "Yes, ma'am, I am working on Josh's scrape book."

"Good, you make sure you take care of Damon. He is a good young man. I told him to keep his mind on his goals and off them hoes if he wants to do right by you." I laugh at Ms. Waters, "What are you laughing at, girl? You know I am right. How is Josh doing?" I replied, "He is happy, Ms. Waters,"

"Good, well let me give you some tea on that fat hog Gina. As soon as Damon pulled up to your old townhouse, her ass wobbled over to him. Gina was in his face; any closer her tongue would be down his throat. You need to watch that nasty stank fat hog. You know she always had a crush on Damon."

"Ms. Waters, I'm not worried about her,"

"Well, you should be. She slept with Damon while y'all were dating."

Shanel frowned, "What did you just say, Ms. Waters?"

"Girl, you heard me. Damon told me that a while back, he said it was a terrible mistake. That is the night your mother told him you were out with some guy named Mike,"

I looked puzzled, "Mike, I don't know anybody by that name,"

"Well honey, that is what your crazy ass two-tone mother told Damon." Said Ms. Waters

I slam my hand on the table, "Damn, my mother did a lot of conniving crap behind my back,"

Ms. Waters continued to dish the tea. I was not expecting to hear no mess like that. "That is not the only thing she did; I can recall when your mama tried to pay Damon to break it off with you. She said that you were a no-good tramp sleeping around with different men to make ends meet." I pushed my son's scrapbook to the side, "Ms. Waters, you know that's not true,"

"I know that, but your two-tone trifling mother, she made it very convincing to Damon," said Ms. Waters

I begin putting Josh's scrapbook away, "why are you telling me all this now?"

She said, "Because you need to know how trifling people can be. You are such a sweet young lady, Shanel. I wish I had you as a daughter. I don't understand why God never sent me a good man. I waited for a long time for my man to come. Now it's too late. The Doctor told me that I have cancer, and it has spread all over my breast like wildfire. That's why I have been smoking my weed."

I gasp, clutching my chest. "No, Ms. Waters, I can't believe what I'm hearing,"

She said, "Well, believe it, honey. I can die any day now since I rejected chemotherapy. Hell, who wants to look half-dead? Not me, as long as I have my special medicines, I'll be just fine. Oh yeah, one more thing, your daddy and I used to sleep together,"

I asked, "Ms. Waters, are you high?"

She replied, "Yeah, but I know what the hell I'm saying because Jada is my fucking daughter,"

I get up from the table in disbelief. "What the hell are you talking about, Ms. Waters?"

She firmly said, "I am talking about the truth, Shanel. The truth you need to hear, before I leave this awful place that causes me so much hell. Your daddy took Jada away from me, and gave her to his cousin, he was sleeping with. Yeah, your daddy was a nasty bastard and a sick man just like his daddy."

I said, "I can't right now,"

She shouts through the phone, "Well, you better soak it all in, because I am on a roll. I will not take secrets to my grave and go to hell for nobody. So, you better remember everything I am telling you." I am clutching my stomach, "I feel nausea." Ms. Waters laughs, "That's how I felt every time I slept with your daddy." I became frustrated with her on the phone. "I don't want to hear this crap no more; I'm hanging up the phone."

"You do that, but the truth always has a way of coming out." Said Ms. Waters, I hung up without saying goodbye. I sit at the table in shock, "My life is getting more complicated. The donor they call daddy is straight-up evil. Why lord, why did I have to be in a family like this? All the wrongdoing that the donor they call daddy did, he should have been punished, a long time ago. Now, Damon is another story; I will handle him later. I knew this happiness was too good to be true. I can never be happy. I just want to be free from everybody and live on a private island.

Chapter 17

Jada calls Pastor Dobbins on lunch break, "Good afternoon, Pastor Dobbins; how did it go with Shanel?" He chuckles, "Everything went well; your sister will be in attendance tomorrow morning."

Jada became excited, "Thank you so much, Pastor Dobbins. I will let Sharon know." She hung up with the Pastor and called Sharon; she answered on the second ring, "What's up, Jada?"

Jada asked, "What are you doing?"

She sighed heavily, "I am sitting at my desk, reviewing over reports. I am trying to find the discrepancies before my board meeting next week."

Jada said, "Well, I just got off the phone with Pastor Dobbins,"

"Well, what's the verdict?" asked Sharon.

Jada smiles, "Shanel will be at the church tomorrow morning."

"Excellent, "Is she bringing Damon?" Asked Sharon

Jada replied, "I don't know why?"

Sharon's tone changed harshly, "Because he doesn't need to be at our family function; he's not married to Shanel."

Jada said, "Well, if he does come, do not start no shit. Remember, we are trying to get our family back on the right track." Sharon replied, "Whatever."

Jada said, "I'm not playing; our family needs help,"

Sharon replied, "Okay, okay, okay, I hear you, Jada."

Jada asked, "So, are you going to the hospital today?"

"Hell yeah, I want to make sure Daddy sees my face when he opens his eyes." Said Sharon

Jada chuckles, "You have flipped the hell out, haven't you?" Sharon sucks her teeth, "I'm just angry with daddy's ass; I hate him right now."

Jada shakes her head in disappointment, "Don't let daddy control you."

Sharon becomes annoyed with Jada, "How is he controlling me? He is laying up in the bed pretending to be in a coma; daddy needs to stop faking and wake the hell up so he can face his wrongs." Jada sighs heavily, "Girl, you are so full of hate that you cannot comprehend anything I am saying to you. Do not let your hate for Daddy limit you from moving forward to a future of greatness." Sharon replied, "I am sitting at my desk looking at the view from the window. My life is great."

"Okay, have you forgiven Daddy?" Asked Jada

She said, "No, I'm waiting for him to wake up so we can talk,"

"What if daddy doesn't come out of his coma, then what Sharon?" she becomes firm with her sister, "Oh, he's coming out of that damn coma Jada, believe that!"

"What if he doesn't Sharon? Will you still be able to forgive Daddy?"

She hesitated, "I believe so."

"You answered that with so much joy. Sharon, you and I both know that you can't forgive Daddy. Why don't you talk to your mama about the situation," Sharon becomes hostile, "For what? She left me before my sixteenth birthday,"

Jada is completely baffled, "I thought…"

"Well, you thought wrong, Jada. That is why I was so close to Daddy. Where is your mama? I do not hear you talking about her too much."

"Uh, s-s-she good," said Jada. Sharon smirks, "I hit a nerve; come clean, Jada."

"Okay, Sharon, my mama is in a mental hospital," She laughs, "Girl, stop lying," Jada cries, "You think that's funny bitch?" Sharon's laughter stops quickly, "Oh, you are serious?"

She replied, "Yes, heifer."

"Oh, Jada, I'm sorry; what happened?" she sighs. "I don't know exactly, but I heard bits and pieces from my aunties over the years that it had something to do with Daddy."

Sharon sucks her teeth, "I wouldn't put anything past Daddy anymore; I feel like I don't even know Daddy."

"Please don't discuss my mama's situation with nobody," said Jada.

"Uh, that goes both ways, sis. Let me ask you a question; since you are harping on me about Daddy, can you forgive him?"

She replied, "Yes, I can forgive him, I don't want the devil controlling my life. I want to be free and happy, not suppressed, depressed, or oppressed. Look, my lunch break is over, and I did not have a chance to eat. So, I will be grouchy all day long."

"Hold up, Jada, how do you think everything will go tomorrow with Pastor Dobbins?"

She replied, "I don't know, but I hope we have a breakthrough; if you think about it, none of us had perfect parents; we were no better than Shanel. Well, at least I had my mama for almost ten years."

Sharon sighs, speaking with envy, "Good for you, but she not here now, is she?"

Jada said, "Damn, you evil grinch, trying to steal what memory of joy I have of my mama."

"What joy do you have, Jada? Your mama is in a mental hospital. She probably doesn't even remember you anymore." Said, Sharon

Jada yelled into the phone, "Don't get mad at me because your mama left your ass, get mad at daddy. He knows damn well he had something to do with that too." Sharon shouted! "Bitch," before hanging up in Jada's face. Jada chuckles, "I must have hit a major nerve."

Sharon angrily grabs her purse from the bottom of her desk drawer. She takes a deep breath before calling her cousin Melissa; she answers on the first ring, "Girl, your cousin Jada get on my damn nerves."

Melissa said, "Uh, you know I'm at work, right?"

She replied, "I do not care; take a break. I need somebody to vent to right now."

Melissa said, "Okay, let me walk outside to the patio." Sharon walked out of her office informing her assistant she is leaving, "Uh, Wendy I'm not feeling good. I am taking the rest of the day off.

She said, "I hope you feel better."

Sharon smiled while on the phone with her cousin Melissa. "Are you outside yet?"

Melissa replied, "Almost; I'm walking downstairs to the patio now." Sharon got into her Lexus. Melissa said, "Okay, I'm clear; now what's so damn important that I need to go on break?" Sharon drives off from her job, "That damn Jada can be a handful; she interrogated me about forgiving my Daddy. Hell, it is going to take me some time to forgive my dad for what he did. I will forgive him, but it must be on my time."

Melissa said, "Why don't you save all this anger for the family counseling tomorrow morning with Pastor Dobbins? By the way, do you know if Shanel will be attending?"

"Sharon sighs, "Yeah, she's coming, damn if these people don't stop driving like it's Sunday, I'm going to run their ass off the road,"

Melissa said, "Girl, calm down. Oh, I heard Daryl is bringing his mama to the counseling session,"

"Good, I believe Daryl knows all my daddy's dirty secrets," said Sharon.

Melissa asked, "How do you know for sure? My mama said her brother-in-law was a private man. She never felt comfortable around him are the family.

Sharon said, "True, but did you hear what Daryl said, Melissa?"

She replied, "he said a lot of things."

Sharon chuckles, "Girl, I promise you just as bad as my sister Jada. Do you recall he said he always eavesdrops on my daddy's conversations?"

Melissa said, "Okay, so what?"

Sharon shakes her head, "Damn Melissa, you aren't too bright, are you?" Melissa sighs, "Is this leading to something?" Sharon chuckles, "I'll keep it to myself."

"Melissa gets irritated, "You made me take a fifteen-minute break. You better start talking, heifer," Sharon pulls up to her luxury townhome, sitting in the car talking to her cousin, "Let's just say I believe Daryl has an agenda. If he's bringing his mama to the family counseling, you better believe my little brother is going to bust my daddy's ass wide open."

"I don't know about that; it would make Daryl just as guilty as all of us." Said Melissa.

Sharon replied, "No, not really, knowing my daddy, he probably threatening his ass. Come to think about it, why do you think Daryl was never around us? Hell, Jada, and I were not even invited to my daddy's wedding,"

Melissa said, "I remember asking Uncle Darren why you and Jada were not at the wedding. He would never give me a straight answer."

Sharon frowns, "That's because he was doing evil shit back then."

Melissa said, "I have to disagree with you cuz. I think the reason why Daryl wasn't around his sibling is because he was younger than y'all."

Sharon chuckles, "Poor naïve cousin Melissa."

Melissa is annoyed, "I'm about sick of you Sharon, "I'm about to hang up on your ass,"

Sharon laughs, "Hold up, cuz, have you reached out to Shanel?"

She replied, "Uh, no, I'm waiting for tomorrow to release the volcano on her ass. Have you called your sister?" Sharon chuckles, "Girl, you a mess, and no, I don't know what to say to Shanel. If I had the freakin power to turn back the hands of time, I would."

"Shoulda, woulda, coulda, you can't, so we need to move forward, and I need to get back to work; talk to you later, girl." Sharon hangs up with her cousin exiting out of her car and walking toward her townhome.

Chapter 18

I am still sitting at the table in shock at what Ms. Waters said on the phone earlier. I had to snap out of my deep thoughts, looking at the time. "It's after one, I need a drink to swallow that hard pill that Ms. Water gave me today." My phone rings, and I glance at the number. If it's essential, they will leave a message. The phone rings again, and I glance at the number again. I think for a second. Oh, that could be the learning center where Josh is. I answered on the third rang, "Hello." A soft, masculine male voice asked for me, "Shanel."

"Speaking, who is this?" I asked firmly, "Daryl, you haven't recognized my voice yet?"

"Sorry, so why are you calling me?" I asked,

Daryl cleared his throat, ""My mama just got word that Daddy had woken up. He's in stable condition; he damaged his right ear and missed his temple by an inch. I don't know what Daddy was thinking.

I replied, "Okay, but why must you inform me? The Donor you call daddy could care less about you updating me on his recovery."

Daryl sighed, "Because you are his daughter."

I said, "I understand your logic, but really, I'm good."

He chuckles, "He couldn't even carry out his suicide, correct?"

I asked, "Why are you so bitter?"

He said, "I should be asking you, why aren't you bitter for what daddy did to you?"

I sigh, "I'm surprised, I thought you had a great life living with the donor you call dad,"

He replied in an angry tone, "I was living with a Demonic force named Darren. Can you imagine having to live a lie every day of your life while people worship your daddy like he was some kind of God?"

I asked, "Are you going to participate in the family counseling tomorrow?"

He replied, "Yes, I am," Daryl paused, "Are you as happy as I am that Daddy shot himself?"

I was caught off guard, "I can't answer that, Daryl," he sighed, "Well, I wish he was dead."

My mouth dropped to the floor, "Oh my goodness, that was very harsh, Daryl."

Daryl said in a harsh tone, "he treated my mother as if she was a slave; I'm talking about the cotton-picking slave that is in the hot sun begging for water type of shit. So yeah, I have every right to feel the way I do about our daddy."

"Trust me, I understand, but wishing death on the donor you call dad is not your revenge. Let God deal with him. Is your mama coming tomorrow?"
He sighs, "Yeah, maybe this will help all of us to heal from the pain that Daddy has caused this family. I know Sharon and Jada..." I interrupt Daryl, "Please, I don't want to hear their names right now."

He said, "Oh, trust me, Shanel they feel like horse shit. Remember our previous conversation when I told you that our sisters were at the house when daddy shot himself?"

I replied, "Yeah, I remember. What happened?"

"Sharon was trying to prove Jada wrong about something concerning you." Said Daryl

I'm puzzled, "Huh?"

Daryl continued talking, "I really don't know all the details, but I was snooping around through Daddy's stuff in his office to find more information on our daddy. Let's just say he should have been in jail for all the shit he has caused a lot of people."

I frown, "Trust me, I'm aware of some of the donor y'all call daddy dirty deeds,"

"Well, I have all his dirty deeds in my file that I have been waiting to use on his ass, and tomorrow seems to be the perfect day. It's going blow everybody's minds away, even poor Pastor Dobbins and my mother." Said Daryl

I hesitated, "Uh, Daryl, never mind," he asked, "What's on your mind, sis?"

"I was thinking maybe we can…you know, go to lunch or something."

He chuckles, "Shanel, I'll take any offer from you. Just let me know when."

I smile, "I'll get back to you soon."

He asked, "You promise, Shanel?" I chuckle, "I promise,"

"Okay, I'm going to hold you to that promise, sis."

I said, "See you tomorrow morning Daryl," I hung up with my brother, sitting at the kitchen table, thinking about my life and the direction it was going. Lord, I can either go forward, be happy, and prosper or stay in the past, having a pity party every day of my life. The front door opens. Damon calls my name; I sigh before answering him, "I'm in the kitchen," he walks into the kitchen with bags from the store, and Josh follows behind his daddy with one bag. "You're back early," Josh runs to me and hugs me. "Mama, I had lots of fun today. I have a new friend named Terry, he's nice." I smiled, "Good, I'm happy for you, baby."

Josh asked, "Mama, may go outside and play with my new friend?"

I asked, "He's over here now?" Damon nods as he puts away the groceries, "Mama, may I please go outside and play?" I get up from the table to walk Josh to the front door. A young, slender Hispanic woman wave at me making her way to my stairs, "Hi, I'm Catalina, Terry's mom. We live across the street from you,"

I smiled, "Nice to meet you,"

"I was wondering if Josh could go to the park with Terry; it's behind your home." Said Catalina. I glanced at her son and then back at Catalina, "I will take care of Josh as if he were my own son. I 'm just happy Terry has a new playmate; as you can see, there are not too many kids in the neighborhood." I agreed, "Okay, Josh, you better be on your best behavior."

"Yes, ma'am," Josh runs toward his new friend. I frown, "What the hell did I just do?" Damon walks up behind me, "You let your son enjoy being a kid. You can't shelter Josh in the house for the rest of his life; let the boy have fun with his new friend." I roll my eyes at Damon walking back into the house. He's baffled as he closes the front door, following behind me. I walk through the kitchen to the backyard on the deck; I sat down on the patio furniture, watching my son playing with his new friend between the trees. Damon follows me outside, sitting across from me. He stares at me, "What's with the fucking attitude?" I glance at Damon, then back at my son on the playground. "This is not the time to talk right now."

Damon said, "Yes, it is. Josh is not here. Now, what's wrong with you?"

I said, "Okay, did you sleep with Gina?" Damon cleared his throat, "What the hell?"

I replied, "You heard me. Did you sleep with Gina, yes or no?" Damon held his head down in shame, taking a deep breath. "Yes, I did, but it was a mistake; who told you?" I frown, "Why did you sleep with her?"

He said, "Shanel, can we not talk about this?"

I replied, "Hell No! We need to put it on the table and deal with it; as you said earlier, Josh isn't here."

He frowns, "Okay, I slept with her because of your mother. She told me you were seeing my homeboy, Mike."

I shake my head, "Well, did you think to ask your homeboy before you slept with Gina?"

He said, "No, I was pissed the hell off. As I said, it was a mistake." I sighed, "A mistake that could have been prevented if you would have taken the time to come talk to me about the situation unless that was an excuse to fuck her." Damon glared at me, "Are you kidding me right now? Why are you rehashing all this old shit up in the first place?"

I replied, "I was talking to Ms. Waters," Damon got up from the table and walked over to me. He pulls me up from the chair, looking directly into my eyes. "I'm not going to even lie to you, but I will tell you this, I made mistakes in my life that I'm not happy with. I'm not perfect, I am trying my fucking best to be a good man to you, so please don't hold that over my head." Damon leaned toward me and gave me a soft kiss on the cheek. My body tingled, and I pulled away from Damon quickly. I said, "Okay, okay you thirsty, I know I am." I walked into the house to grab a bottle of water out of the refrigerator; I gulped that water down quickly. I forgot how soft his lips were. Stop it, don't fall into that trap again. Damon walks into the house, "Are you okay?"

I replied quickly, "Yes," My cell phone rang. I walk to the kitchen table, looking at the number, "I'm not going to answer that phone," Damon walks over to the table to see the number, "Yeah, it's best that you don't talk to your mother right now. We can go shopping when Josh returns home from playing with his friend."

"Okay," I walk back outside to keep an eye on Josh. Damon walks out the front door without saying a word. I continued watching my son as I enjoyed God's beautiful portrait.

Chapter 19

Sharon walks into her daddy's hospital room, "So you finally woke up, huh? I'm surprised nobody called, but that's okay. I was sitting in my townhome about to chill when I thought to myself go to the hospital and torture my evil ass daddy, so I'm here. I know you can talk. Your doctor has already informed me that your injuries are healing, and you will be released from the hospital on Friday. You can ignore me all you want, but I'm going to be on your ass Daddy. So, I will sit here all day until you speak to me." Darren looks up at the ceiling, taking a deep breath, "I've already apologized; I'm not going to keep apologizing to you about the same thing repeatedly."

Sharon glares at her daddy with an evil eye, "How about you apologizing to Shanel?"

"Has she even been here to see me?" asked Darren. Sharon got up from the chair, standing over her daddy, "Oh yeah, she even overheard her mother, Ms. Howard talking to you about plotting to kill her." Darren coughs, "You got to believe me, Sharon. I didn't want no part of that plot on Shanel's Life," "That's not what Ms. Howard said, Daddy."

"The hell with her; she crazy."

Sharon paused, "Oh… so what are you, Daddy?" he replied, "I'm not perfect," she frowned at him, "When did you finally discover that before or after you shot yourself?"

"The Bible says to forgive Sharon," she points her finger in her daddy's face, "Don't be telling me what I need to be doing; you lost that right." Darren clears his throat, "Let's get something straight, young lady. No matter how you feel toward me, it was my sperm that brought you into this world. So, you will always be a part of me. You can never erase that."

She cried, "You're right. I can't, but I can make you suffer," Darren sighed, "Sharon, you're wasting your time hating me; why don't you put that energy into forgiving me and yourself? If you don't watch out, you are going to let your anger trap you in a place you don't want to be." Daryl and his mother walk in on Sharon and Darren, "Is everything okay?" asked Deborah. Sharon frowned, wiping her tears. "No," Daryl sat in the chair, looking toward Sharon. "Fussing at Daddy isn't going to solve anything. You must find a way to deal with your anger toward him."

"Daryl, he needs to pay for what he did," Deborah sat next to her son, nodding in agreement, "Believe me, daddy will pay for everything he has done, but it's not your call to make on how daddy is supposed to pay for his wrongdoing, it's God decision, and you need to respect that." Sharon wipes away the tears rolling down her face, "But it's not fair."

"Life isn't fair, hell I wish daddy was dead my damn self, but it wasn't in God's will," Darren looks toward his son frowning, "Look, Sharon, vengeance is the Lord, not yours, now go home and pray, relax in the lord, sis." Sharon sighed, "I can't. I'm too angry to even go in pray." Deborah shakes her head, looking toward her husband. Darren turns away from his wife, looking at the ceiling. The nurse enters the room to check on Darren as Sharon and Daryl are in deep conversation. "One thing I can say is out of all daddy children, Shanel should have the most anger toward daddy. He didn't even acknowledge Shanel unless it was to bash her. She's handling the situation better than you."

Sharon asked, "How do you figure that?" Daryl replied, "Because she is not at the hospital daily and fussing with Daddy like you." Sharon grabs her bag from the chair, glaring at Daryl, "Fuck you, and your daddy." Daryl and his Mama look at Sharon in shock; they weren't expecting that from Sharon; she walks out of her daddy's room, angry. She reached for the cell phone in her bag to call her sister Jada. It went straight to voice mail, and she hung up without leaving a message. "I need somebody to talk to." Sharon walks from the hospital to her car, looking around before entering her Lexus. She tries to call her sister Jada one more time, "Damn Jada, where the hell are you at?" She cranks up her car with Tevin Campbell, always in my heart, blaring through her speakers. As Sharon was about to drive off, Ms. Howard knocked on her passenger side window. Sharon was startled; holding her chest, she rolled her window down, "I didn't mean to startle you, Sharon," "What do you want, Ms. Howard?"

She smirks, "How is your daddy doing?"

Sharon scowled at Ms. Howard, "Why don't you go see for yourself? His wifey and son are visiting him right now, so you may want to return later." Sharon rolls up the window before Ms. Howard can say anything and drives off. Ms. Howard storms into the hospital to go see Darren, "I don't give a damn about Darren's wife; what is she going to do to me?" Ms. Howard chuckles as she gets on the elevator, "I'm going to be on my best behavior," she gets off the elevator and walks toward Darren's room. She smiles as she enters his room, "Hello Deborah, how is your husband, my ex-sleeping partner," Daryl grimaces at Ms. Howard. Deborah leaves her husband's room; Daryl runs after her, "Mama! Don't let this bitch run you out of your husband's room." Darren frowns when he sees Shelly; she walks up to him and kisses him on the forehead, "You really know how to pick'em. She is one ugly, weak, insecure woman, Darren."

He coughs, struggling to talk, "Will you get the hell out of here," Shelly smirks, "I will do no such thing, you the helpless ass that's bedridden right now, so I'm in control. I can do a lot of evil things like slap the hell out of you like this," she slaps him so hard that it echoes in the room, Darren chuckles, "That doesn't hurt, my face is numb you evil witch." Shelly frowns, "I hate you."

"Ditto. Why are you here anyway?" asked Darren. She smiled, "I came to torture you since you couldn't carry out one order to kill your daughter,"

"I'm not going to do that; since you want her dead, why don't you kill her, Shelly?"

She replied, "Are you crazy? I am not going to jail for that bitch of a daughter; I have too much to lose. You, on the fucking other hand, have nothing to lose. You have an ugly wife, your son looks gay, and your deacon status is over," Daryl walks into his daddy's room as Shelly runs her mouth. "Bitch, if you don't get your ass out my daddy's room disrespect his family, I will get Shanel to beat the hell out of you. Now get out!" Daryl grabs her bag and throws it out of his daddy's room. The nurse gets up from her station when she sees bag fly out the room. "Lord, I'm about tired of this family. Heal Mr. Darren Nelson so they can leave this hospital," Shelly laughed, "Wow, is that all you got, Ms. Thang?" The nurse walked into Darren's room, "I am tired of dealing with this immature family. If you all can't act like respectable grown adults, I will have the entire family ban from the hospital, now try me if you want to." The nurse walks out of the room. Shelly blows a kiss at Darren, "I'll be talking to you later, my love," he frowns, she laughs walking past Daryl, "Kiss, kiss, I forgot you don't do women," Daryl spit in her face, "I do like women not whores like you," Shelly shouts, "you nasty bastard!" she runs out Darren. Daryl walks up to his daddy's bed, shaking his head, "Do you see what your evildoing has caused upon this family?" Darren looks up to the ceiling. sighing, "I won't keep apologizing to you and your sisters. If God can forgive me, then you all should forgive, and that's all I have to say. Now you can leave. I need my rest?" Daryl glared at his daddy with so much hatred, "What about your wife, the woman who stuck by your sorry ass?"

Darren grunts, "Boy, you're lucky I'm in this hospital bed,"

"What are you going to do? You can't hurt me no more than you already have." Said Daryl

"If you think that's supposed to make me, feel guilty, then you don't know me son. You can hate me for who I am, but you know what? I don't care; I don't care. I have made my bed, and I'm lying in it. When it comes to my wife, you let me worry about that?" said Darren.

"Well, I guess that's my cue to leave." Daryl mumbles under his breath, "You a piece of work." Deborah walked into her husband's room as her son was leaving. "What did you do to our son, Darren?"

He replied, "Nothing, he was just in his feelings as always. You baby him too much; he needs to grow some damn balls." Deborah throws her bag at her husband. Daryl stands outside his daddy's room, eavesdropping on his parents' conversation. "Are you crazy, woman?" she growls at her husband, "Yes! You have turned me into a mad woman; I watched you and Shelly Howard for years having your affairs on the side, then the woman has the nerve to walk into this hospital acting like she's your damn wife. I'm your wife! I'm the wife who has stood by you through all the conniving, deceitful ways you have done toward the people who loved you. I prayed day and night, hoping you would change back into the man I married. It seems like the more I prayed, the worse you got. Well, I'm tired of praying for a man who doesn't love his family or God. You are evil, Darren, just pure evil with a black heart. I am not going to deal with you are your bull crap anymore. I'm tired of pushing your trash under the rug and being the laughingstock of this family. I'm filing for divorce first thing in the morning." Darren begins coughing and laughing at the same time, "You are crazy if you think you are going to divorce me, woman?" She raises her hands to the ceiling, "You are laying in this hospital bed still trying to control me; your threats don't scare me anymore, Darren. You can kill me, put a spell on me, do what you want. I don't care. My God is bigger and better than you, and I know he will take care of his shepherd." Darren frowns, "I will not give you a divorce."

"It's ways to work around you, Darren," she grabs her bag off Darren's bed, "God will see the family through all the hell you put us through." Daryl dashed down the hospital halls so his mama wouldn't see him being nosy and standing by his dad's room door. Deborah leaves her soon-to-be ex-husband's room, walking to the nurse station, "Excuse me?"

"Yes, how can I help you?" said the nurse. Deborah hands her a piece of paper from her bag,

"Will you make sure that y'all get a hold of Shelly Howard when Darren is discharged from the hospital on Friday?" The nurse smiled, "Yes, ma'am." Deborah walks down the halls of the hospital like a queen that has found a throne again.

Chapter 20

I'm sitting at the kitchen table making a grocery list for Damon for tomorrow. Josh walks in the kitchen, "Mama, may I have a bottled water?"

I smile, "Go ahead, don't make a mess either."

"Yes, ma'am," Josh went to sit outside on the patio with his daddy. My cell phone rings. I get up from the kitchen table and walk to the counter next to the refrigerator to answer my phone, "Hey, Shanel."

"Hey, Ms. Waters, how are you feeling?" I walk into the den and flop on the sofa; she sighs, "I'm okay,"

She said, "I have so much I want to say to you," I chuckle, "Ms. Waters, you've said enough already."

She replied, "Oh no, the hell I haven't either. You don't know your family," I begin smiling, "Ms. Waters, what are you doing tomorrow morning around ten o'clock?"

She replied with a light cough, "The same thing I'm doing right now, smokin' and chokin' on my weed." I laugh, "Ms. Waters, I don't know what I'm going to do with you?"

Her voice cracked, "Pray for me, baby. I need serious prayer."

I sadly replied, "I can do that. I need you to be ready around nine o'clock tomorrow morning,"

Her voice went from sentimental to aggressive, "For what?"

"You'll see, I think you'll be a big help in my counseling with Pastor Dobbins tomorrow," Ms. Waters begins fussing on the phone, "Shanel, I'm not stepping foot in no damn church; those church folks love to judge people like me. Oh, hell no, kiss my ass, Shanel. I'm better off staying my ass home smokin' my weed." "Ms. Waters, how you going to ask me to pray for you and you cussing me out?"

Ms. Waters said, "The church is evil,"

I frown, "Hold up, Ms. Waters, the house of the lord is not evil; it's the devils that come into church pretending to be saved, giving the true men and woman of God that are saved a bad name. You must understand that the church is open to pretenders, deceivers, liars, and so on. You can't turn nobody away from the house of the lord."

Ms. Waters sighs, "Well, I guess so, but if one of those little hussies says one thing out their mouth about me, I'm going to bring out a can of fuck you up." I chuckle, "You can't be cussing in the lord's house. Ms. Waters, I don't know where it will be held in the church. I need to check my e-mail tonight; you just be ready when we pick you up in the morning." I hung up the phone and sat on the couch for a minute. I almost forgot what I was doing. I get up from the couch walk into the kitchen, "I thought y'all were chillin' on the patio." Damon is at the table with Josh adding their suggestions to the grocery list. "We were, but Josh wanted to come in and add pizza to the list. Who were you talking to?" asked Damon.

I replied, "Ms. Waters, I invited her to the family counseling," Damon paused momentarily, "Why would you do that? Do you know how wild that woman is? She will be kicking everybody's ass in at that meeting, including the Pastor.”

I laugh as review over the new grocery list, “Ms. Waters is going to be all right, but this list needs some changes. I will not be buying candy, beer, and pizza.” Josh frowns, getting up from the table and walking to the den to watch TV. “Well, to be on the safe side with Ms. Waters, y’all need to pray for the angel to pour buckets of the blood of Jesus over Ms. Waters’ mean ass.” I laugh, “You better stop talking about her like that. When I’m in counseling tomorrow, can you go shopping?”

Damon smiles, “Yeah, I can do that. So, are you getting nervous with the entire family coming together tomorrow?” I sigh, “I don’t know how to feel, Damon?”

He replied, “I can understand; you don’t know what to expect from this family counseling.”

I walk to the window, looking at the pretty sunset, “You’re right about that. I miss sitting in my chair looking out my window; this sunset is beautiful.” Damon walks up behind, “Yeah, it is; God is the best artist in the world.” I nod in agreement. I turn to Damon, looking him directly in the eyes. I smile, “Excuse me,” he moves to the side for me to walk past him, and I walk back into the kitchen while Damon joins his son in the den to watch TV. I asked, “Hey guys, what do y’all want for dinner?” Damon shrugs his shoulders, “I don’t know. Whatever you cook is fine with me.”

Josh asked, “Mama, can I have the pizza Daddy bought me today?”

“Yes, you can, baby,” Damon chuckles, “Can I have a pizza too?”

I said, "Uh yeah, get up and fix it yourself. While you are at it, fix your son pizza, too."

"I thought you were fixing us dinner," said Damon.

I chuckled, "No need for me to cook; you can microwave your pizza."

"That's cold, Shanel, real cold," I laughed and sat at the kitchen table looking through my cell phone. Damon walks into the kitchen to cook dinner for him and his son. I sigh, "I need to start deleting numbers from my phone; I don't talk to half of these people anymore."

Damon said, "Why don't you go upstairs and enjoy your bedroom."

I replied, "I can't enjoy myself right now. I have a million thoughts running wild in my head. I want this family counseling ordeal to be done and over with."

Damon put his son's pizza on a plate, cutting it before serving it to him. "It's going to be okay. You are making the situation bigger than it is. Look don't put too much thought into it; just go with an open mind. Don't get discouraged and give up like your daddy almost did." Damon calls Josh into the kitchen to eat his dinner; he comes into the kitchen smiling, "Thank you, Daddy." Damon cell phone rings: he reaches into his pocket to answer his phone, "What up, D-Man?"

"When are you coming back to Cali?"

Damon walks into the living room, "Saturday after my cousin's funeral."

"All right, you handle dat, 'cause when you get back to Cali, we've got seven artists lined up. I'm talking about A-listers paying good money for us to produce their tracks," Damon smiled excitedly, "That's what's up, D-Man."

He said, "You hold it down in the A." Damon hung up, putting his cell phone in his pocket, and returned to the kitchen. "I smile, "Who was that?"

He replied smiling, "My business partner," I got up from the table, "When are we going shopping? I don't have anything to wear tomorrow."

"He replied, "We can go after Josh, and I get through eating." I smiled, "Okay, I'll put my shoes on." I ran upstairs to get my shoes. Josh pouts, "Daddy, I don't want to go shopping. Can I go over to Terry's house and play with him?"

Damon said, "Terry and his mama may be busy doing their own thing today."

Josh replied, "No, Daddy, Terry, and his mama are always bored watching TV, so he will be happy for me to come over and play. Can you go ask Ms. Catalina, please, Daddy!" Damon chuckles, "First, you have to run that by your mama." I come downstairs, "Run what by me?"

"Josh wants to go to Terry's house while we go shop." Said Damon.

I smile at my son, "If it's okay with Catalina, then it's fine with me." Josh jumps around in excitement, and the doorbell rings. I look at Damon, and I ask, "Who would be ringing our doorbell?" Damon shrugs his shoulders and tells his son to be quiet as he walks to the door. The doorbell rings again; Damon looks through the peek hole; he sighs in relief, opening the door, "It's Catalina and Terry," they come inside the house. "I'm sorry to bother you, but Terry wants to know if Josh can come over and watch a movie with him." Josh comes running out of the living room to the front door. Damon chuckles, "We were just about to come over to see if Josh could stay with you while we go shop."

"Sure, go ahead," said Catalina.

I replied, "Thank you," Josh hugged me and his daddy before leaving out the front door. I watched my son walk away with his friend. Damon, close the door, "Are you ready to go shopping?"

I replied with excitement, "Yeah, I'm ready. What is my limit?"

He said, "Get whatever you want; I don't care." I smile, "you said the wrong thing. I'm going to spend all your money." He chuckles as he grabs his keys off the key holder, "Let's go," He follows behind me, mumbling under his breath, "Help me, lord." I chuckle, "I heard you big head."

Chapter 21

It's Wednesday morning; Josh comes into his mommy's room, jumps in her bed, and gives her a big kiss on the cheek, "good morning mommy," I wake up smiling and yawning, "Good morning to you too, sweetie." Josh sits besides, "Daddy told me to tell you to get up and get ready for your meeting today. Mommy, can I walk with Terry and his mommy to school this morning? I already asked Daddy, and he said it was up to you, so can I, Mommy? Please," he begins hugging and kissing me on the cheek, and she smiles, shaking her head. "Boy, you're a mess. Okay, go take a bath and brush your teeth."

He smiles, "Mommy, I already did that after I ate my breakfast,"

"What did your daddy fix you for breakfast?" he replied, smiling, licking his lips, and rubbing his tummy. "Pancakes and bacon," the doorbell rang, and Josh jumped out my bed and ran downstairs. I get out of bed, rush to put on my housecoat, walking downstairs. Josh's friend Terry was standing in the living room with his mother, "good morning, Shanel,"

I smile, walking toward Josh, "Good morning, Catalina,"

She said, "I am here to pick up your little man for the learning center. I wanted to ask if Josh can go with Terry and me to the pizza place today." Josh looks at me, smiling, I replied, "Yeah, it's okay." Josh hugs me and his daddy. "You have a great day at school." Said Damon. Catalina and the boys out the door. I walk into the kitchen while Damon locks the front door. I poured myself a glass of juice,

Damon asked, "Shouldn't you be upstairs preparing for your family counseling?" I sipped on my juice, "I should, but I don't want to be a part of my family shenanigans." I finished the rest of my juice. "Shanel, are you scared?" I put my glass in the sink, "No, why should I be scared?"

He replied, "Because you are hesitating." I sighed, "I'm not scared. I don't know what to expect from this so-called family counseling."

Damon said, "Well, you can't back out now. You already told Ms. Waters to be ready this morning. You are overthinking; why don't you go upstairs and get ready." I frown at Damon. I walk upstairs, talking to myself. "Black, I should wear all black. It represents how evil and conniving my family is." I look inside my shopping bags for her black pants and blouse to match. Damon cell phone rings. He answers on the third ring, "Son, I have some terrible news: your auntie cremated your cousin Dee's body without the family knowing." Damon flops down in the kitchen chair, "she did what?"

His mother said, "You heard me, son,"

Damon paused, "what the hell, why would she do something so thoughtless?"

"His mother sighs, "Damon, this shouldn't be no surprise. Your auntie has always been that way."

Damon said, "Mama, but that was her son. You would think that triumphs over money."

"I hear what you were saying, son, but not all people think the way you do, so you just have to accept people for who they are and treat them accordingly."

Damon firmly said, "I hope Karma comes back on your sister and mess her up. Because of her, I couldn't pay my last respects to my cousin. What did she do with his ashes anyway?"

His mother takes a deep breath before answering her son softly, "She flushed them down the toilet." Damon shouts through the phone, "she did what!" I came rushing down the stairs to see what was going on. I see Damon sitting at the kitchen table, banging his fist on the table in anger with tears rolling down his face. "Mama, you mark my word, auntie is going to pay for what she did to my cousin."

His Mother said, "Damon, you let God handle your auntie. He knows how to do it better than you." Damon wipes his tears away, "Mama, I got to go," Damon hangs up with his mama, looking at me. "Are you okay, Damon?"

He replied, "You look like the Grim Reaper,"

I chuckle, "Good, that's what I was going for,"

"Why?" asked Damon.

Shanel smirks, "Because I want to bring their spirits down like they did me for the majority of my life," Damon shakes his head, frowning at me. So, you just going to play right into your family fucking hands?" I roll my eyes at Damon, "no, I'm not," He said, "Then go change into something that represents I'm happy despite what my family did to me over the years. Don't let them have the upper hand over you. It's time for you to come out this rut that your family has put you in." I gave him that look, "Damn, I promise that look will make a man run from you. That's probably why you didn't get much love from the fellows." Said Damon, "Shut up, Damon, now what's going on with you?"

He sighs heavily, "Nothing, I'm good. You need to be getting ready."

I replied, "I will, but who were you fussing with on the phone?"

Damon put his phone in his pocket, "Shanel, let's get you to your family counseling on time. We can deal with my situation later."

I said, "Okay, are you sure?" Damon motions for me to go upstairs. I rushes upstairs to change, "What am I going to wear now?" I look through my shopping bags. Damon stands by the stairs shouting, "Put on your red pantsuits!" I grab my pantsuit out the bag, "this is too much red I need to tone it done," I reach for my black blouse and begin getting dress. I rushed into the bathroom to do something to her hair. Damon shouts, "Come on Shanel we still have to pick up Ms. Waters!" I slip into my red and black six-inch heels rushing downstairs meeting Damon at the bottom of the stairs. "Is this better?" he frowns, "You could have fixed your hair instead of putting it in a curly ponytail."

I said, "Uh, no, I don't want to look like a puff ball all day. Curly hair can be a hassle, especially in this summer humidity." Damon smiles, "I'm just making sure you dressed on point." I chuckle, "Hold up, what do you know about style? You still rocking clothes from the eighty and ninety." We walk out the front door, "that's okay because the eighties and ninety's clothes are coming back in full effect." Damon opens the car door for me, "Keep dreaming," We both got in the car, Damon put in his Troop cd. "Who is Troop?" I asked. Damon cranked the car up, backing out of the driveway. "What! Girl, stop playing. Everybody knows who Troop is, spread my wings, Mamacita, All I do is think of you." I smile, "Oh, they were good, but New Edition was great." Damon laughs, "Please, Troop and Ready for the World were the best great groups."

I chuckle, "Let me stop you right now so you don't continue to embarrass yourself." Damon laughs, "I know my group. You need to get on board to enjoy real music,"

"I know my group too, and New Edition is the best group next to The Jacksons. Were any of your groups compared to the Jacksons?" Damon laughter fades away, "okay, okay you win,"

I chuckle, "Now repeat after me, New Edition is the best."

Damon replied, "You crazy, I'm not repeating that shit,"

I said, "Don't hate, appreciate my boys. I don't play about New Edition. I have all their albums, tapes, and CDs."

Damon frowns, "You crazy."

"I'm just a dedicated fan; nothing crazy about that." We pull up to the old neighborhood to get Ms. Waters. Gina and her husband are sitting on the porch this morning, playing spades, and drinking beer with some of the neighbors. Damon parks in front of Ms. Waters's townhouse, and as soon as he gets out of the car, Gina calls his name, he waves at her. She gets up from the card table walking across the street toward Ms. Waters townhouse. She was so busy trying to get to Damon that she didn't even see me sitting in the car. Damon comes walking back to the car with Ms. Waters in his arms. Gina walks up to Damon, "What the hell is your fat ass doing in my yard?"

Gina rolled her eyes, "Hey Ms. Waters, uh Damon, what's going on with you? You don't come over to the crib no more and chill with us." Before Damon could say anything, Ms. Waters butted in the conversation. "He doesn't want to be around your dirty fat ass, he has a woman that he loves now get out my yard." Damon helps Ms. Waters into the car, "Gina walks to the car and sees me sitting in the passenger seat. Her eyes almost popped out of her socket. She waves at me, then walks over to Damon, talking to him. Ms. Waters begin talking to distract me from getting out of the car and whooping Gina's ass. "How are you doing Shanel?"

I replied, "I'm okay. I just wish Damon would bring his behind on so we can make it to the church on time." Ms. Waters rolls her window down, "Damon, leave that hog alone so we can go." Gina's smile fades. He said, "I'm coming Ms. Waters." Gina begins walking off, and Damon gets in the car without saying anything. "So, what the hell did Gina want?" Damon acted like he didn't hear me. Ms. Waters said, "Damon, did you hear what Shanel asked you?"

He said, "I did,"

"Then answer her," I frown, "Don't worry about it, Ms. Waters, they probably made another date to screw each other." Damon begins to chuckle as he drives out of the old neighborhood, I asked, "Can you stop by the breakfast café."

He replied, "Yeah," I shook my head, thinking about Gina and Damon. I mumbled, "There's more to their relationship than what he's letting on." He said, "Shanel, I have already told you about that situation. Why are you letting Gina push your button."

I replied, I am not giving in to her. You need to put your foot down with her." He sighs, "Gina she is the least of our concerns. My focus is you and Josh."

Chapter 22

Sharon and Jada pulled up at the same time as Pastor Dobbins, "Good morning," said Jada.

"Good morning, ladies."

Melissa pulls up as Pastor Dobbins unlocks the educational building next to the church; Jada and Sharon walk in behind him. Shanel, mother pulls up in the church parking lot sitting in the car for a minute before getting out the car. Melissa walks into the educational building, "Good morning, everybody."

Pastor Dobbins replied, "Morning, Melissa," Jada and Sharon smiled. Melissa looks around the room, "Where is Shanel?"

"Sharon replied, "I don't know, but I hope she shows up," Shanel's mother walked in without speaking.

"Good morning," said Pastor Dobbins. She frowns at the Pastor, "Why are we having a meeting in the Sunday school building?" Pastor Dobbins smiles, "We hold all our family counseling in the educational building."

"Okay, I was just asking, no need to get an attitude," said Ms. Howard

Jada and Sharon chuckled, whispering to one another, "This is going to be interesting," said Sharon.

Jada replied, "Tell me about it," Daryl and his mama walked in, he was toting a notebook. Sharon and Jada glanced at each other, then back at Daryl, "Good morning." said Daryl, his mama, waving at everybody. Pastor greets her with a smile.

Sharon waits for Daryl to get settled, "So what's with the notebook?"

"He smiles, "I will let you know in due time, so where is Shanel?"

"I don't know," said Jada.

Ms. Howard smirks, "Knowing my daughter, she won't show up." Jada cut her eyes at Ms. Howards. The pastor looks at his watch, "It's ten-thirty; we need to begin our session and pray that Shanel attends."

"Sharon and Jada sat next to each other on the right side of Pastor Dobbins. Daryl and his mother sat on the left side of Pastor Dobbins. Ms. Howard sat across from Sharon, and Melissa sat next to Daryl's mother. Everyone sat at the round table in silence, not knowing what to expect from the family counseling. Pastor Dobbins took off his glasses, wiping them with a handkerchief; the door opened, and everybody frowned when they saw Ms. Waters. "What is she doing here? She is not family," said Sharon. Ms. Waters smirked and sat beside Ms. Howard, "How are you doing, Shelly?" Ms. Howard froze.

I walked in the door with a box with bags from the breakfast café. I had cups, a gallon of orange juice, and sweet tea. "Good morning, I'm sorry I'm late, but I had to stop and get breakfast." Pastor Dobbins smiled, "the lord answered my prays because I was stravin marvin." I chuckled and set everything on the table. I sat in the middle of the round table facing everyone. Pastor Dobbins said,

"Okay, before we get started, let us bow our heads: Heavenly Father, we come to you in Jesus' name, asking that you bless this family counseling to be a breakthrough for everyone. I ask that you direct this family on the path of righteousness and touch their heart. I plead the blood of Jesus over everyone sitting at this table, from the crown of their head to the sole of their feet. Bless the hand that prepared this breakfast that sister Shanel blessed us with. In Jesus' name, we pray, amen.

Now, before we get started, I do have a few rules. We will use a baton in this session; whoever has the baton will be the only one speaking, and there will be no interruptions. When that person is finished talking, we will take turns voicing our opinions. This will not turn into a Jerry Springer showdown. Do I make myself clear?" Asked Pastor Dobbins: everybody at the table agreed, "Okay, since we are clear on the rules, let us enjoy this wonderful breakfast. I'm going to pass the baton to Jada first," said Pastor Dobbins, Jada poured herself a cup of sweet tea. She nervously took a long sip before speaking. "Um, I don't know really what to say. I just wanted to get the family together so we can discuss the deep-rooted issues that have been affecting us for years. So, I will pass the baton to Shanel," said Jada. Ms. Waters glanced at Jada and then back at me. "Me," I cleared my throat, "Okay, um, what am I supposed to talk about, Pastor Dobbins?"

He wiped his mouth before answering, "Whatever you feel you need to release from your heart, whether it's good or bad, but no cussing." I nod in agreement; Sharon grabs a chicken biscuit while Jada and Melissa are drinking their sweet tea. I sighed heavily, looking around the table at my family. I began fidgeting with my fingers glaring at my mother eating a chicken biscuit. I glanced at the Pastor, who was eating the hell out of his hash brown. I cleared my throat for the second time. "I'm just going to be straight up with everybody. I don't like my family." Jada looks at the Pastor; Ms. Howards chuckles, shaking her head. Sharon almost choked on her tea. "Why do you feel this way toward your family Shanel?" asked Pastor Dobbins.

I frown, "The donor they call Daddy," Daryl chuckles.

"What about your Daddy? May I ask why you call him The Donor?" asked Pastor Dobbins.

"My Daddy has been the biggest issue in my life, the man shoots himself in the ear missing his head by an inch, and he is still alive. How in the world does he survive that? I believe my dad and the rest of my family are here to torture me. As you say, Pastor Dobbins, everybody has a purpose in life whether it's good or bad; in my case, it's bad." Ms. Waters nods in agreement, "My mother, the evil woman who embraces me with so much hate. I never knew a mother could hate her child with so much passion." I glance at my mother, shaking my head. "Pastor Dobbins, I have so much that I want to say, but my thoughts are not coming together." He said, "Take your time, don't force it, just let it flow naturally." I take a deep breath. I said, "My sisters and my cousin Melissa, I can't trust them. They treated me so horribly. I felt like a trash can. They would just dump all their negative inputs on me almost every day." I begin to cry, "Every time I was about to climb out the trash can, here they come again, dumping more of their negative inputs on me again. I stopped going to church, but I stayed in my bible and prayed. It was hard on me sometimes. I just wanted to die, because nobody could feel the pain, I had bottled up inside of me. Nobody can understand the hurt of not having a family beside you in your time of need.

Nobody could understand how it felt to be a failure trying to take care of your child on a minimum wage paycheck. You know, I used to make $7,500 a month and pay my tithes, and I could not understand why God allowed me to lose everything. I did everything right, but then I realized today that I still had hate for each one of you except Ms. Waters. I was going to wear all black today to represent death; that's how I feel when I'm around you all. I realized God was not punishing me; he was teaching me how to be a loving, forgiving, humble person so that he could bless me. It's not the material things that make you blessed. It is the love, the joy, the peace, the long-suffering which I have endured. The gentleness, the goodness, the faith, the meekness, and the temperance that make you blessed. I just realized that every man and woman must bear their own cross like Jesus; that's what I had to do. I should have been content with my tribes and tribulations, not complaining to God why am I going through this. I realized God protected me from a lot of things seen and unseen; he's had my back from day one. A man couldn't help me, but that bible did. I thought I was going to tear into each one of y'all, but God had another plan this morning FORGIVE! That's what we need to do; there is no need to go into the past to rehash all the negative energy. Let's move forward with truth, forgiveness, and healing. To answer your question, pastor he is my donor, not a dad."

I look around the table and see my family with tears rolling down their faces, except my mother. I hand the baton back to Pastor Dobbins; he looks around the table before responding, "Shanel, I must say the spirit of the Lord is upon you this morning, forgiveness is the key to getting this family back on the right track.

Everybody nods in agreement with the Pastor except for Ms.

Howard. "I'm sorry, I don't agree," said Ms. Howard. She held her hand out for the Pastor to pass the baton. Sharon glared at Ms. Howard as her tears streamed down her face. "First of all, Shanel was a mistake; she should have never been born. I wish I could rewrite my life. I would have gotten that abortion." Shanel's head went down, "She messed up my life and her Daddy's; he said she cursed the family. I had to raise this devil child by myself. I hated her back then, and I hate her even more today. I thought about giving Shanel up for adoption, but I didn't want a good family cursed with my evil seed. I did mention I hate her with a passion, and I feel sorry for the man who marries her. That's all; how do you like the way I express my forgiveness." Ms. Howards hands the baton back to Pastor Dobbins, laughing.

He said, "Lord, this has taken another turn. Does anybody want to address Ms. Howard?" Jada held her hand out for the Pastor to pass the baton. "I want to say Shanel, I received everything you said, and I would love to work on forgiveness and healing, but I need to get this off my chest, Ms. Howard, you are evil, just pure evil. How could you treat your daughter like that? You and our Daddy don't have any remorse for the things you did to this family. You and my Daddy have divided and destroyed this family for years; it ends today. I can't take back the things I did and said, but I can make it better by repenting for all my wrongdoings against my sister Shanel and the rest of my family. I am not innocent. I'm just as guilty as my Daddy and Ms. Howard; I apologize, Shanel. Maybe after the forgiveness and healing, we can come together as loving sisters, taking it one day at a time, getting to know each other without the negative input from others."

Jada hands the baton to Pastor Dobbins; Sharon smiles at Jada.

Ms. Waters holds her hand out for Pastor Dobbins to hand her the baton, "My name is Jade Waters," Daryl's eyes bucked wide, "I have known Darren Nelson since I was eighteen. I thought he was nice, but his wickedness came out when he met Shelly Howard." She frowned, shouting, "You don't know me like that old lady! You better watch yourself!" Pastor Dobbins, said in a calm, firm voice, "You need to hold your comment after Ms. Waters finishes talking Ms. Howard."

She rolled her eyes at Ms. Waters, "Honey, I know more than you think. I was talking to Shanel on the phone about my past. Since I won't be here much longer, I decided to let the cat out of the bag. I'm not as old as people think I am."

Ms. Howard chuckles. Ms. Waters gives her a nasty look, then continues, "I'm just fifty years old, the life I chose to live made me age before my time. See, Darren Nelson and I used to shack up together for 15 years before Shelly came into the picture. I was pregnant when he left me for two-tone. That's my nickname for Shelly. Darren told me that I wasn't going to keep the baby. I thought he had lost his ever-loving mind. Honey, as soon as I gave birth to my baby girl, he took her away from me like Celie's Daddy did her in the movie Color Purple." Shelly chuckled, shaking her head as she continued talking, "he gave my baby girl to his cousin, whom he was also sleeping with the entire time we were shacking up."

Daryl looked through his notebook; Sharon and Jada glared at Ms. Waters. "Darren was something; he thought he was some kind of God, playing with people's lives. Shanel, don't hate me, but your Daddy helped you get that townhouse across the street from me," My mouth dropped to the floor, "as a matter of fact, he owned the building you were staying in." Ms. Waters looks across the table, smiling at Jada. "I thought I was going to take my secret to the grave, but I decided to clear my mind, body, soul, and spirit from everything good and bad. I don't want God to be mad at me on judgment day."

Ms. Waters sighs. Daryl stands up, "I need to stop her from saying what she's about to say." Everybody is looks baffled, "I don't think it's the right time to reveal this information in front of everybody, Ms. Waters."

Ms. Waters rubs her hands together, looking around the table. "This is the right time, Daryl. I may not have another opportunity. Valena Nelson is not Jada's mother; I am." Jada glared at Ms. Waters; in shock, tears flooded her eyes. Jada cries, "You are lying, my mother is Valena Nelson. You are a liar."

Daryl sighs, "No, she's not, sis." Everyone at the table gasped except for Shelly, who was smirking. Daryl continues explaining to his sister. "Jade Waters is your biological mother," Ms. Waters hands Daryl the baton, "The woman who raised you was Daddy's cousin. As Ms. Waters said, he was sleeping with her along with Darren's Daddy, our granddad, like father, like son.

I was told by Daddy's sister Darla, Valena's mother, Geneva, fell on hard times. They had to move in with Granddaddy and Grandma. Since Geneva had no money to help around the house, she had to keep her legs open to her uncle, our granddaddy Darren Sr. The sad thing about this situation is that Darren Sr. made his son Darren Jr. have sex with Geneva, too. Then when Geneva took ill and died at the age of thirty-five, Granddaddy began having sex with Valena when she was at the tender age of thirteen. She got pregnant by Darren Sr. He gave her an abortion himself in the outhouse, which messed her up from being able to conceive any more children. He kept having sex with her then he brought Darren Jr, our Daddy, into the circle keeping up his Daddy tradition. When Grandma found out what her husband was doing, she put rat poison in his food. I asked Auntie Darla why didn't grandma do anything to our Daddy Darren Jr? I was told she was in denial; she thought the world of Darren Jr, so Valena took the power into her own hands and blackmailed our Daddy. She was going to go to his church and let them know that he's been raping her since she was thirteen if he didn't get her a baby. So that's how Jada ends up being Valena's daughter." Jada's eyes are flooded with tears; she gets up from the table rushing to the bathroom vomiting. Sharon and Melissa ran to go check on her. Ms. Howard claps her hands, "now this is the best family counseling I have ever been in, we should get a reality TV show and make some money." Shanel gets up from the table and walks toward her mother and slaps her in the face. Pastor Dobbins rushes to Shanel, pushing her out the door; Ms. Howard laughs, rubbing her face, "It did not hurt, but do you see what I mean? Shanel is evil; that is the devil's daughter." Ms. Water glares at Ms. Howard, "What, Jade? You want to slap me too? What do you and Daryl think y'all going to prove by spilling the beans on Darren? It did not change anything; it is just going to cause more confusion in the family."

Daryl replied, pointing his finger toward Ms. Howard, "See, that is where you are wrong. It helps bring out the deep-rooted issues we have been struggling with for years. It is out; no more pushing trash underneath the rug or dumping negative input in the trash to hide; it is over, Shelly."

In the meantime, the Pastor is conversing with me, "I know I made myself clear when I said I did not want to have a Jerry Springer showdown. You did not have to slap your mother in the face, Shanel. Do not let her make you lose your peace with God."

I frown, "I apologize, but she had that coming."

He said, "You need to learn not to get on the same level as the devil; you need to elevate your spiritual growth. Now, we will go back inside and be on our best behavior, okay."

I smile, nodding in agreement. Pastor Dobbins and I walked back inside the educational building; I walked past my mother and sat in my seat. "I just want to apologize for slapping you in the face, Mother." Ms. Howard smirks, "I don't accept the devil's apology." I glance at the Pastor, then back at my mother. I smile, "Well, as long as I clear my conscience, I am good."

Ms. Howard laughs, "The devil loves having the last word." Ms. Waters points at Shelly, "You are the devil." She laughs as Pastor Dobbins gets up from the table to check on Jada. Ms. Howard looks over at Deborah, "You look pitiful, Mrs. Nelson." Daryl glares at Ms. Howard, "Leave my mother alone. She is not messing with you." Deborah smiles, "As a matter of fact, I am happy, blessed, and highly favored!" Ms. Howard frowned, "Whatever." Sharon and Melissa walked back to their seats. Sharon gave Ms. Waters a dirty look and then looked in Daryl's direction; he said, "What Sharon?"

She replied, "You wrong for putting Jada's business out in the opening like that, and Shanel is dead wrong for bringing this woman to our family counseling." I stood up from my chair and walked over to my sister, Sharon.

"You better watch out; she good for slapping people in the face," said Ms. Howard,

She stands up, ready to defend her face, "You do not have a right to tell me whom I can bring to this family counseling. Ms. Waters is Jada's mother. Whether you like it or not, Jada needs to put her pride aside and get to know her biological mother before she loses her."

Sharon sucked her teeth; I stood face to face with Sharon. "Girl, you better be lucky; I promised Pastor Dobbins, I would behave myself." I stared my sister down. Sharon backed up from me and sat down; I walked back to my seat. Ms. Howard comments, "Oh, so you don't slap her in the face; she must be scared of Sharon." I frowned, "You trying to get underneath my skin," Ms. Howard asked, "Whose idea was it to have this family counseling? I thought we were supposed to focus on the old, deep-rooted issue. Not bring up new crap, geez!" Ms. Water turns to Shelly, "There is nothing new about me being Jada's mother; you and Darren thought this would never come out? Well, the devil is a lie." Shelly frowns, shaking her head.

The Pastor and Jada walked back into the family counseling. Her eyes were puffy, and she sat back in her seat with her head down, "Okay, family, we have less than two hours to go before we end our session. Who has the baton?" Daryl raises the baton, "are you finished?" asked Pastor Dobbins

"No sir, I have more information to reveal," the Pastor mumbles, "Lord, guide us in the right direction."

"Jada, I do apologize about how the truth came out concerning your mother," she kept her head down, "Everyone at this table knows that I am the youngest and only son of Darren Nelson. I endured so much pain from this man. I watch our dad and Ms. Howard, a.k.a. Shelley, manipulate people. So, it hurts me to let Jada and Sharon know about their mother. Well, the woman who raised Jada, no disrespect to you, Ms. Waters." Sharon stood up quickly, shouting, "I already know what happened to my mother. She ran away from her responsibilities."

Ms. Howard smirks at Sharon, "wrong," the Pastor motions for Ms. Howard zipped her mouth, "Why don't you shut up, Ms. Howard?! You are being immature and rude," said Daryl. Sharon sat down looking confused.

Ms. Howard replied, "And you need to stop lying about you not being gay." Everybody frowned at Ms. Howard comment. "Ms. Howard, you can say whatever you want, but you are barking up the wrong tree. I love women, always have, and always will." Sharon commented, "What, no comeback." Ms. Howard sat back in her seat, rolling her eyes at Sharon. "Now, getting back to the matter at hand. We all know that Darren, our Daddy, put Valena Nelson into a mental institute after she threatened to tell the Pastor what he did to her if he did not give her fifty thousand dollars in cash. Now you know Daddy was not having that, so he did what any evil person would do. Taking revenge into his own hands, he drugs and admits her into a mental institution. Now, as far as Sharon's mama goes, your mama did not run away. She took her life in front of Daddy and Shelly at his apartment that he used to share with Shelly." Sharon gets up from the table looking at the Pastor with tears rolling down her face, "I can't do this, Pastor Dobbins."

"Yes, you can, and you will; you cannot keep running from these deep-rooted issues. It is time to heal and move on, Sharon." Said

Pastor Dobbins.

Sharon cries, "Pastor, I know you want to help my family by putting everything out on the table, but the person who is responsible for all our pain in the hospital. I am just so angry at Daddy for what he did to me, my family, and now my mama, my poor mama." Sharon began crying harder, with snot and slob coming out of her mouth. Daryl passed the baton back to Pastor Dobbins; I reach for the baton again, wiping my tears away. "I am confused, Daryl; you said that Sharon's mama killed herself in front of the donor they call Daddy and my mama in the old apartment that they used to share. We were teenagers when Sharon's mama ran away, so when did she kill herself?"

I handed the baton to my brother, and he replied, "It was before Sharon's sixteenth birthday. Daddy kept that apartment for his one-night stand with different whores. Shelly used to go back from time to time riding the devil." I chuckled, shaking my head and glancing at my mother. "Auntie Darla told me Natrice and our daddy were messing around again. She thought he was going to leave my mama and marry her. Sharon's mother, Natrice, got a rude awakening when she caught our Daddy between Shelly's legs. Natrice went to her car to retrieve her gun and shot herself in the apartment right in front of them, hoping Daddy would feel guilty." Shelly smirked and added her two cents. "Darren didn't even stop having sex; he said I'm not going to waste a good orgasm on no dumb whore." Sharon jumped out of her seat, but Pastor grabbed her just in time. Sharon shouted, "I am going to kick your ass, bitch!" Pastor walks Sharon outside. I stood up, shaking my head; I snatched the baton off the table, pointing in my mother's direction. "You could have kept your two cents to yourself. Sharon just found out that her mama committed suicide after all these many years. Sharon did not even get a chance to pay her last respects or bury her mama. You and the donor they call Daddy took that from her. Both of you are so evil; then you have the nerve to smirk about it. I am furious right now. If you weren't my mother, I would beat you down with this baton. Lord knows I am trying to keep my composure." Jada shook her head and said, "Our family foundation is evil; we have evil blood running through our veins." Shelly shuns her daughter and Jada, looking through her phone. I said, "Ms. Deborah, you have not said anything. Do you want to address anybody?" she shook her head no; I looked in my cousin direction, "Okay, what about you, Melissa?"

She replied, "I have nothing to say; I am still trying to engross the information exposed this morning." I sat back in my seat, reaching for a chicken biscuit. "I guess we will wait for Pastor Dobbins and Sharon to come back inside, in the meantime I'm going to scarf down this chicken biscuit." Everybody sat in silence. They heard Sharon fussing outside with Pastor Dobbins, "I cannot believe my brother did this to me. He should have come to me about my mother's death. How am I supposed to face my family now, Pastor Dobbins? With this shame?"

He replied, "The same way Shanel, Jada, and your brother are doing right now, facing it head-on. Now, we are going to go back inside. I do not want to hear any more profanity out of your mouth, do I make myself clear." Sharon nods and walks back in, wiping her tears. Pastor Dobbin walks in behind Sharon, not looking so happy. He takes the baton off the table. "I am very disappointed in this family. It seems we just wasted our time; you just want to fuss and fight. I will not tolerate this nonsense anymore or I will end this family counseling. Now, does anybody want to take the baton?"

Sharon holds her out for the baton, "I just want to apologize for my outburst toward Ms. Howard. As far as my brother, I just want you to know that I am angry with you Daryl for not coming to me first about my mother's death. I do not like being caught off guard like that." She wipes tears rolling down her face, "And to my cousin Melissa, what happened to you leashing the volcano out on Shanel for kicking you out of her house?" Ms. Howard chuckles, "She's scared Shanel is going to slap that pretty little face of hers." I glanced at Melissa, "You need to address me, Melissa?"

She holds her head down, and Sharon sighs, "Girl, you weak just like your mama." Melissa frowned. I held my hand out for the baton, "I need to address Jada," I looked at her sister. "You need to get to know your biological mother; she has breast cancer, and she does not have too much time left on Earth. I should be angry with the donor you all call Daddy because I wasn't a boy; he punished me. If my Daddy would have accepted me, maybe my mother would have loved me, and my sisters would have treated me better. So please get to know Ms. Waters before it's too late." Sharon begins crying; you could feel hurt and pain pouring out. Daryl asked for the baton; he said, "Shanel, I never hated you; I wanted to get to know you; it was Daddy keeping me away from you." he sighs, "I have a notebook with all of Daddy's dirty laundry that he wrote down. I made copies for everybody to read so you can get a clear idea of how our Daddy, Darren Nelson, operates. Pastor, I'm telling you this will help my sisters and Ms. Shelly Howard, a great deal. The enemy has had us in bondage for much of our life; it's time to take our freedom back from the devil."

Pastor agreed, "That's right, Daryl, you all have been going through adversity, but God has been there for every one of you, except Shelly Howard, she definitely serves the devil." She smirked, "Now it's time to turn on your spiritual ear, family, so that you can listen to God. Jesus is the only one who can make you free from bondage, so stop fighting with each other. I want you all to start talking to one another and become the family God wants you to be. Every one of you showed up looking for help. God put you all in the right place this morning, and I believe he will heal this family from the inside out so you all can finally rest in Jesus. Don't let the devil delay your blessings any further. On that note, I think you should read your brother's information on your Daddy and meet back on Saturday at the same time." Said Pastor Dobbins.

Sharon smirked, "Yeah, because our Daddy will be released from the hospital on Wednesday; he wasn't badly injured."

Deborah scowled and stood up, shouting, "Friday!" Everyone at the table was startled, Sharon cuts her eyes at Deborah, "Huh?"

She said, "He will be released on Friday," Sharon frowned, "My bad, Deborah." Deborah held her hand out for the baton. "I'm so sick and tired of you all disrespecting my soon-to-be ex-husband, your Daddy. He may not have been the best person, but he has done a lot for you and Jada. He has sent you two to college, and bought you new cars, and townhomes, that he has paid off. Daryl had to work his behind off to get an academic scholarship. Your Daddy didn't give Daryl and Shanel the same opportunity as you all. Now I see why you two are weak. You two could not handle the tribes and tribulations that Shanel and Daryl had to endure from your evil Daddy." Ms. Howard sniggered, pointing her finger in Deborah's direction, "Sit your ass down; Daryl and Ms. Waters are so busy putting everybody busy on blast, that they forgot to mention you. Ms. I'm blessed and highly favor dirty laundry."

Deborah glares at Shelly as she sat in her seat, "You need to mind your business."

She smirked, "Well, your tutti frutti son should have thought about that before he opened his mouth. Pastor Dobbins, should I tell your wife's little dirty secret."

He replied, "Ms. Howard, you need to leave, well enough alone, this is about your family."

Ms. Howard chuckles, "Since everybody wants to put me on blast about my past, let's talk about why you didn't go to the hospital to see Deacon Darren."

Pastor Dobbins' voice became firm, "I am warning you, Shelly, shut your mouth." Deborah gets up from the table, "Where are you going sister Holy? It would be best if you stuck around for this, Daryl…" Deborah grabs the gallon of tea throwing it at Ms. Howard, drenches her face and clothes. She shouts, jumping up from her seat, "You crazy heifer, what is your problem!?"

Deborah shouts, "You are Shelly! You have wrecked my home with your manipulation. I am tired of you. I wish your ass just would die!" everybody's mouths dropped to the floor. "Mama, don't let her bother you." Ms. Howard laughs, reaching for napkins to wipe herself off. "I was just going to tell Daryl to get a blood test so he will…" Deborah shouts, cutting her off in the middle of her sentence. "Stop it, Shelly!" Daryl glanced in his mama's direction, "Mama, what is she talking about?" She has tears rolling down her face; she clears her throat. Shelly laughs, "Go ahead and tell him, Mrs. Highly favored in the lord, let's see if the Almighty welcomes your ass into the kingdom now." Daryl looks at his mama, "Tell me what's going on, mama?" She breaks down in tears, "I can't, baby."

Sharon and Jada are confused, looking around the room to figure out what the hell is going on. I shake my head in disgust, looking at my mother, "Don't be shaking your head at me; Deborah is the stupid one." Daryl shouts, "You shut up, and leave my mama alone!" Shelly shouts back, "Your mama needs to be honest and tell the damn truth!" Pastor Dobbins stands up from his seat, speaking in a firm voice, "All right, that is it; I am tired of telling grown adults to behave themselves; this family counseling is over."

Jada looks at her phone for the time, "No, it's not. We have forty-five minutes left, Pastor Dobbins." He glanced at his watch, cleared his throat, and sat down in his chair, nervously fidgeting with his thumbs. Deborah set the baton on the table; Sharon reached for it looking in her direction, "I don't know what's going on, but whatever it is will be brought to light eventually." Shelly added her two cents, "Why wait, let it be known now." Sharon cut her eyes at Shelly, "Uh, I have the baton right now, so stand down, Ms. Howard."

She mumbles, "It's Shelly, smart ass." Sharon shuns her off with her hand, "Deborah, I hope you can come to grips with whatever secret you are holding back from the family and move on, in peace." Deborah wipes her tears avoiding eye contact with Sharon. Shelly chuckles, looking at Deborah, "She's not your mama, Daryl." Deborah looks at Shelly angrily. "Yeah, I said it; what the hell are you going to do about it?" Deborah looks at her son, then back at Shelly, she gets up. Deborah says, "I am leaving, Pastor Dobbins; you can fill in the blanks." As she left the building, Daryl got up from the table following behind his mother. Shelly burst out into laughter, "I finally won. I finally got that goody-two-shoes." Sharon throws the baton toward Shelly, missing her face by an inch. "You missed Heifer." Sharon and Jada went outside to check on their brother. Melissa is sitting at the table quietly sipping on her tea. I shake my head, "You didn't win, mama; you lost." She laughs snapping her fingers at me. "Trust me, I won, Pastor Dobbins; you need to fill in the blanks. I bet you didn't think it would involve you and your wife. Man, I'm telling you, this would be a good-ass reality show."

"Mama, shut up; you are getting on my last nerve. You lucky I'm a good person, or you would be in the hospital fighting for your life." Shelly gasps, "Did you hear her, Pastor Dobbins? She threaten my life. I told you; Shanel is evil." Pastor Dobbins cleared his throat before speaking, "Shelly Howard, you are something else; Shanel just speaking her mind." Shelly sighs, shaking her head.

Sharon and Jada walk back inside the educational building with their heads down, walking to the table. Daryl and his mama walk in shortly; Daryl breathes heavily, "Mama is going to share her truth with us." Pastors' Dobbins sighs, rubbing his head. Shelly smirks, "Well, it's about time. Pass her the baton so she can speak the truth." Deborah snaps, "Shut up, Shelly; if you pass me the baton, I'll use it to beat some sense in your head." She laughs, rubbing her hair, "Somebody's angry," Deborah sighs heavily. "Okay, um, of course, you all know that my soon-to-be ex-husband, you all Daddy and Uncle was far from perfect. He had a lot of extra-marital affairs. Well, one of his affairs was with First Lady Dobbins." Deborah broke down in tears, looking at her son. "Which brought a child into the world that I have been raising as my own." Daryl froze; he couldn't open his mouth to speak. Shelly Shouts, "Hot damn! What do you have to say about that?" Daryl was shocked; he fell out of his chair and hit the floor. Shanel, Sharon, and Jada rushed to see if he was okay. Shelly chuckles, "Chile, I think you done killed him. He couldn't handle that truth." She laughs, looking toward Deborah. Pastor Dobbins asked, "Is he okay?"

"Yeah, he is breathing." Shelly gets up from her seat and walks to the bathroom laughing. "I'll get a cup of water." Pastor Dobbins sighs heavily, taking his handkerchief out of his pant pocket and wiping the sweat beads forming around his forehead. The sisters kept shaking Daryl to wake him up. Shelly returns with a cup of water. "Move out the way," she throws the cup of water in his face. Daryl wakes up gasping for air. "What happened?" Sharon passed me a napkin from the table, I wiped my brother's face. I helped him back in his seat.

Jada walks back to her chair, giving Shelly the evil eye. "This is all your fought, Ms. Howard; you should have let well enough alone." Doesn't the good book say somewhere in one of those Johns, That the truth shall set you free? I am just compiling with the Holy word." Deborah corrects her, "It's John: 8 v 32. 'And ye shall know the truth, and the truth shall make you free." Shelly cut her eyes at Deborah. "Well, it's the same thing."

She said, "No, it's not; you need to beware of the leaven of the Pharisees." Shelly looked at Pastor Dobbins and asked, "What does that mean?"

"Hypocrisy, that's another topic for another day. We need to get through this day." Said Pastor Dobbins. Daryl is looking at his mama, "can you tell me what happened?"

"I'm not your biological mother; First Lady Dobbins is." He looks at Pastor Dobbins, "So, my Daddy?" He shakes his head, "No, Darren is still your Daddy; my wife cheated on me with your Daddy.

Now, let's move forward." Daryl holds his head down, mumbling. "I didn't see that coming." He sighs, fighting back his tears, "So, did your wife, my mother even care about me?"

Pastor Dobbins replied, "Daryl, my wife has moved on, and you need to do the same. Deborah is your mama now." Can I at least meet my biological mother?" Pastor Dobbins looks at Shelly, "See what you started, look Daryl; you need to find a way to deal with this without involving my wife. We have finally got our marriage back on track. I don't need no more added past problems to destroy my marriage again." Shelly laughs, "Pastor Dobbins, you are not being forgiven as the good book says. It's not his fault that he came into the world from an adulterous relationship. Let him get to know your wife; I mean his mother." Daryl holds his head down, then looks up, glancing at Pastor Dobbins, "You can't stop me from seeing my biological mother. I will take it to court if I have to." Pastor Dobbins frowns, looking toward Deborah.

Sharon reaches for the baton, "We need to bring the man behind all of our problems, our Daddy." Pastor Dobbins clears his throat before speaking, "Well, if he's up to it, then maybe he could join us."

Deborah sighs, "He should be here to address this mess he has caused for his family."

"Oh, he's coming," said Sharon.

Deborah shakes her head, "We shall see."

Pastor Dobbins looks at his watch, "I want everybody to stand up holding hands. I want to say a few words before we pray: this family needs to separate and heal. You all need to have one-on-one time with God so he can mend all your broken spirits. Now bow your head." Pastor begins to pray, and Shelly looks at everybody, frowning, becoming impatient. Before the prayer ended, Shelly let loose Sharon and Daryl's hands and left the church. Sharon and Daryl grab each other's hands. Sharon smirks, shaking her head. The pastor ended his prayer by asking everybody to hug one another; I quickly hug my brother Daryl to avoid hugging my sisters. Daryl hands his sisters copy of their Daddy journal. Jada walks over to Ms. Waters, they exchange information, and Jada calls out to me. I turn to Jada, "Yes."

"If you don't mind, I'll take Ms. Waters home." I glance at Ms. Waters, then back at Jada, "Are you okay with that Ms. Waters?"

She smiles, "I am good, call me when you get a chance tonight."

"I will," I take my cell phone out to call Damon.

"Hello."

I said, "We finished; where are you?"

He replied, "I'm in the parking lot waiting for you. I stayed the entire time; I didn't know if you may need a witness." I chuckled, "It went okay," I walked out the door, talking on my phone. Sharon rushed out the door, calling my name with puffy eyes. I turn around, "Yes, Sharon,"

She asked, "Uh, can we talk before our Friday meeting?"

I sigh, "Damon, I need to hang up. Sharon wants to talk; I'll be in the car soon."

He said, "Okay I can see everything, I am behind the pastor's car." I hung up with Damon and walked up to Sharon. I replied, "I think it is best that we wait until the Friday meeting to talk."

She said, "Please, I am sorry for what I did to you."

I sigh, "Sorry, I can't talk to you right now," I walked away from Sharon and walked to Damon's car. Jada hugs her sister, "Stop crying Sharon, you have to give her some time," Ms. Waters walks out of the educational building, "Girl, stop all that damn crying, that's not going to get Shanel's attention."

"Okay, hold up, Ms. Waters, you need to tone that down." Said, Sharon

She looked Sharon up and down, "Let me tell your rude ass something; you will never have a relationship with Shanel, unless you change that funky little attitude. You cannot control this situation; God must heal and mend all the pieces in this family. Hell, you need to heal over the death of your mother." Sharon glared at Ms. Waters and then walked back into the educational building.

"I need to go get my bag," said Jada. Ms. Waters watched Shanel get into the car with Damon; Shelly walks over to Ms. Waters and said, "So you decided to let Jada know the truth? Good for you, but Darren is going to get you for this," Ms. Waters chuckles, looking at Shelly, "Your opinion matters if you matter; get the hint, bitch. Now remove the tissue from your shoe." Shelly cut her eyes at Ms. Waters and replied, "You are a piece of work cussing on church grounds."

She smirks, "I'm standing next to the devil on church grounds, what's your point, bitch?" Shelly walks away in a rage, mumbling to herself, "She lucky I am on church grounds." Damon and I drive up to Ms. Waters. "All right, last chance," she smiled and replied, "I am going to be all right." We smiled and drove off, while everybody walked out of the educational building, saying goodbye. "All right, y'all be blessed and I'll see everyone on Friday." said Pastor Dobbins. Melissa walks to her car without saying anything; Jada frowns. "What's Melissa's problem?"

Ms. Waters sighs, "The girl feels out of place she doesn't know how to relate. Or she is hiding her dark secrets."

Jada frowns, "Her life is good."

Ms. Waters replied, "No, it's not. None of your life is perfect. Her uncle is Darren; there is no telling what he put her through."

"I never thought Melissa had any issues; she was always quiet and happy," said Jada.

Ms. Waters frowns, "Child you are dense; I'm going to have to school your ass, Jada."

She said, "Ms. Waters please keep your two cents to yourself."

She replied with a sassy tone, "Child, please, I say what I mean and mean what the hell I say." Jada walked to her car, and Ms. Waters followed behind her. Sharon watches her sister get into the car with Ms. Waters. She sighs, "Well, at least she has her mother, lucky Jada." Daryl and his mother drive off, blowing the horn and waving goodbye.

Chapter 23

I am lying across my bed reading the Donor they call Daddy journal. Damon walks into the room and asked, "Why were you quiet in the car?" I sigh, "I have a lot on my mind."

He asked, "Like what?"

"What did Gina say to you this morning for your attitude to change toward me?"

He chuckles as he sits in the chair, "She wanted to have a late-night rendezvous."

I firmly asked, "Did she not see me in the car?"

He sighed, "Girl chill, I sat her straight. We are not dating; we are being responsible parents to our son." I shake my head, "You're right, I need to focus on Josh and myself."

He looked confused, "Huh? You lost me."

I smile, "I need to stop sulking around this place and enjoy life."

"First, you need to heal before you can move forward," said Damon.

I replied, "That is what the family counseling is for."

He asked, "So, how did it go today?"

I sit up in my bed leaning against the headboard, "Just as I expected, crying, fussing, etc.

My brother gave us copies of the donor they call Daddy journal for us to read; we suppose to meet back on Friday."

"Well, you better get to reading," said Damon.

I shake my head, "I don't want to continue reading this crap; the donor they call daddy could have set this up. Think about it: he is a cleverly insane man; he is justifying all his wrongdoing. He put this where he knows that nosey-ass Daryl would find it. This man is a great manipulator."

Damon chuckles, "All right, wannabe Maxine Shaw Attorney at Law."

"Whatever; I know the donor they call Daddy is being released from the hospital on Friday. I will go to house with this journal and confront him with this crap."

"Why wait? Let's go to the hospital right now." said Damon.

I asked, "Are you sure?"

He gets up from the chair, "absolutely,"

I pause, "Wait a minute, Josh should be coming home soon,"

"No, he's not. Remember Catalina taking them to eat pizza, now let's go."

"Hold up," Damon sat back down in the chair."

He sighs, "What now?"

I said, "I can't go," he looks baffled, "What you mean you can't go?"

I replied, "You need to tell me why you were fussing on the

phone this morning?"

Looking at the ceiling, He sighs, "I don't want to talk about it right now?"

I asked, "Why not? I'm not going to get mad, trust me."

He looks at me, "Okay, Gina and I slept together two days ago."

I sat on the bed, trying to keep my composure, "Hey, like you said, we aren't dating each other, right?"

Damon kept his eyes on me, "So, are you ready to go visit your Daddy," I replied, "You mean the donor they call Daddy." Damon chuckles, "Yeah,"

I said, "I need to change out of this suit."

"I'll meet you downstairs," I close the door behind him, my eyes beginning to tear up, "Lord, my heart has shattered into pieces; he slept with Gina again. I cannot get mad; we are not dating. Can you remove my feelings for Damon from my heart so I can move on Ca?" Damon is standing by the door, listening to Shanel. He returns to the room, "Damon, I'm changing," I'm standing in my pink bra and panties, "I need to tell you the truth; I didn't sleep with Gina again."

I walk to the bed, grabbing the pillow to throw at him; he blocks the pillow, "Why would you lie to me, Damon?!" I began crying. "You know I'm going through a lot of shit with my family. Why add more fuel to the fire."

"I need to see if you were telling me the truth about me being able to trust you?"

I scream, "Why are you playing games with me?"

He said, "I'm not,"

I flop on the bed, wiping my tears; Damon walks toward me.

"What, Damon?" he sighed as he kneeled, rubbing my legs gently, "I'm sorry, Shanel."

"Stop rubbing my legs," I pushed him away, getting up from the chair; he grabbed my arm. I said, "Let me go," he pulled me into him, hugging me tight, and tears began falling on my shoulders. I try to pull away, but his grip is too firm.

I asked, "Damon, what's wrong?" his tears multiplied by the minute. He wouldn't answer, and I comforted him until he was ready to talk. Damon looked at me and gave me a peck on the cheek, "Thanks, I needed that."

"What's going on Damon?" He took off his shoes and sat on the bed, pulling me to join him on the bed. He asked, "Can we lay in bed and listen to some Jazz right now?" I turned on the radio clock, the sound of French horns, cymbals, and saxophones drowned out the pain in the atmosphere. Damon wrapped his arms around my body holding me tight. He sighs, "I received bad news from my mama this morning, about my cousin Dee. My auntie already cremated his body without the family knowing, and she flushed his ashes down the damn toilet."

My heart dropped to my stomach, "What the what, are you kidding me?"

He cleared his throat, "No, I'm dead serious. It's been bothering me all day. I know he wasn't the most reliable person in the world, but he was my cousin. He didn't deserve that kind of homecoming. Not having closure is hurting me."

"I'm so sorry, Damon; I'm here for you, my love." Damon paused; He asked, "What did you just say?"

I said, "Huh?"

He asked, "What did you just say, Shanel?"

I replied, "I'm here for you." Damon smiles. "My love, was at the end of that sentence." Damon turned to me and softly kissed me on the lips. I almost welcomed that kiss with open arms but pulled back and jumped out of bed. "What are we doing? I'm not trying to get caught in the moment and end up pregnant again. I have too much going on in my freakin' life; I can't bring another baby into this world."

Damon, still lying in the bed, "My bad, he chuckles; I know you love me because that kiss had me shaken in a good way."

I chuckle, "Can you please get out so I can get ready," Damon smiles, looking at me. The doorbell rings. "I'll get it." He runs downstairs to the front door, "Who is it?'

"It's Josh Daddy," he opens the door, Catalina smiles, "Hi Damon."

"Hello Catalina,"

Josh asked, "Daddy, can I stay at Terry's house for a long time?"

"If it's okay with Catalina," said Damon.

She smiles, "It's cool; I'll have him back by six o'clock."

He smiles, "I'm cool with that. Take down my number, 678-555-5555."

Catalina programs Damon's number in her phone, "All right boys, let's go and have fun, see you later." I come downstairs, I asked, "Where is my son?"

Damon closes the door looking in my direction, "he's going to stay over Catalina's house until we get back from the hospital."

I said, "Okay, well I'm ready."

"Alright, let's go handle your business, my love," said Damon. I smiled as he opens up the front door for me.

Chapter 24

Jada sits in the townhouse with her biological mother, Ms. Waters, looking around and smiling. She said, "This is nice; how come your townhouse looks better than my sisters across the street?" Ms. Waters lit up her weed, and she replied, "Because I had a lot of shit on your Daddy, so he made sure I got whatever I wanted."

Jada said, "So you blackmailed him?"

Ms. Waters took a long puff and blew the smoke in her direction; Jada began coughing. She uses your hand to fan the smoke away from her. Ms. Waters replied, "Hell, call it what you want, if I am happy, then he is happy. So, what do you want to know about me, Jada?"

She rubs her hands together, "What made you want to be with my Daddy, Darren Nelson, in the first place?"

"Child, I don't know because he had nothing to offer me; I was just young and stupid."

"So, you didn't love my Daddy?" asked Jada.

She replied, "Nope," Ms. Waters continues puffing on her weed.

Jada frowns, "Was it the sex?"

"Nah, your Daddy was not blessed with the big tool, but he sure did know how to use his tongue if you know what I'm saying." Jada chuckles.

"Do you have any pictures of yourself when you were younger?"

Ms. Waters gets up from her black leather sofa, walking to the closet. Jada patiently waits, looking through her phone. She comes out with a large blue photo album. "Here, you can have that," said Ms. Waters. Jada looked inside the photo album. Ms. Waters said, "Those are pictures of me, my mother and her side of the family." Ms. Waters lit up again, Jada asked, "How much do you smoke a daily?"

She chuckles, "About ten a day," she looks at Jada. "Let's talk about the real reason you're here." Jada sighed and asked, "Did my Daddy really do those awful things to my mama?"

She replied, "Yes, he did; he was a dirty, perverted man, just like his Daddy. They used to fuck the hell out of me almost every day."

"Ms. Waters why do you cuss so much, and why did they rape you like that?" asked Jada.

She replied with such a nasty attitude, "I didn't say anything about no damn rape. Did you hear the word rape come out my damn mouth?"

Jada replied, "No, I am sorry."

She glares at Jada, "Let me school your ass. Your Daddy doesn't love himself or anybody around him. His Daddy took that away from him when he was young."

Jada said, "I am confused, took what away from my dad?" She took another puff, blowing up to the ceiling. She replied, "Love, see your granddaddy shower Darren with material love. He thinks buying cars, homes and breaking me off a piece of change is love."

Jada asked, "What about Shelly?"

Ms. Waters laughs, "You are talking about two-tone; she is his whore; yeah, they have been screwing each other for years. I wouldn't let a man screw me for free. Two-tone Shelly do not get anything but that limp dick every other night from your Daddy. I feel sorry for that wife of his; he only married her because of Daryl. Hell, we had sex the day of his wedding." She smiles with pride; I whipped it on him good that day. Child, your Daddy is evil. He works witchcraft on people to get his way. I stay away from your Daddy, but he sends my checks in the mail to keep me satisfied."

Jada asked, "Why do you call Shelly two-tone?"

She puffs on her weed, "That's what I call mixed bitches I don't like." Jada frowns, getting up from the sofa. "Okay this has been…uh, I need to go." Ms. Waters smirked and asked, "When are you coming back to see me?"

Jada walks to the door, taking a deep breath. She turns to Ms. Waters, kissing her on the cheek. "I am sorry, but the woman who raised me, has passed away. Valena will always be my mother; I will not replace her, no matter what." Ms. Waters chuckles, "Child, I am not trying to replace Valena. I give her credit for raising my daughter. I just asked you a simple damn question: are you coming back to see me?"

Jada has tears rolling down her face, "No." She rushes out the front door to her car. Ms. Waters closes the door behind her. "Oh well, her loss," Jada calls her sister in the car. Sharon picks up on the third ring with an attitude, "What do you want, Jada?"

She asked, "Are you busy?"

Sharon replied, "No, why?"

"What is with all the attitude, Sharon?" she sighs. "Sorry, I'm just upset over my mother's death. It hurts; all this time, I thought she ran away from her responsibilities, not killed herself. The sad thing about the fucking situation is that Daddy knew all this time, smiling in my face. That shit is a hard pill to swallow, I will never forgive Daddy for that."

"Sis, you need to find a way to forgive Daddy."

"I'm not you, Jada; God knows my heart; he'll help me get over this hump in my life. So, how did it go with your biological mother?

Jada replied, "Girl, that woman is a pill; I will take Valena over her any day." Sharon chuckles, "It was that bad?"

Jada frowns, "Girl, she is the worst. I need to release my frustration. Let's go to Noonday Park and walk too clear our minds."

Sharon's cheers up, "By Town Center, we can rent bicycles too. I will meet you there in thirty minutes. Hey, before you go, will you read the journal that Daryl gave us in family counseling?" Jada cranks her car, backing out of Ms. Water's parking lot. "Girl, please, I think it's fake. Why didn't he say anything about Daddy's journal before?"

"Well, I read some of the journals; they're very interesting and you need to read it Jada."

She replied, "I think I'll pass on the journal and the family counseling. I'm going to call Pastor Dobbins tonight."

Sharon asked, "Why?"

Jada replied, "sometimes you just need to leave well enough alone. I don't want to know anything else about our family secrets."

Sharon sighs, "Yeah, you may be right, but I need to see Melissa and Daddy today."

Jada asked, "Why?"

Sharon replied, "Did you not notice Melissa at the family meeting? She was quiet the entire time, stuffing her face. "We need to talk with our cousin."

Jada asked, "Uh, can we do it after Noonday Park? That Ms. Waters stress my nerves." Sharon laughed, "She did what?" Jada laughed, "See what I mean? I'm not making sense; I'll see you soon, sis." Jada hung up with her sister, drove in the car, listened to BBD poison, bopping her head, singing with the song.

Chapter 25

I walked into the donor they call Daddy hospital room with Damon by my side, handing him the journal that Daryl passed out during the family counseling. "What is this, and who is he?" asked Darren.

"I was hoping you could tell me your son handed these out this morning at our family session with Pastor Dobbins," I pointed at Damon. "He is none of your concern."

Darren frowns, "Why did y'all meet with the Pastor?"

I glared at the donor who they call dad, "Do you need to ask that question?"

He replied, "Yes, did it have anything to do with me?"

I raised my voice at him, "Yes! Darren, you were the main topic of our conversation." He frowns, "Why would you do that?" I gave him a nasty look, "We had every right to go meet with Pastor Dobbins. You have destroyed a lot of people's lives, Darren." He shakes his head, "I know Pastor Dobbins had a field day listening to my family bashing me."

"Stop making everything about you. Your children needed to find a way to deal with our deep-rooted issues." He sighed and glanced toward the door. "Who is he?"

I glance at Damon, then back at the donor, who they call dad, "Don't worry about him. I want to know about this journal." Darren flips through the journal, frowning, "What the hell?! Daryl passed this out to who?"

I replied, "To everybody in the family counseling, so is this true?" Darren stared at the journal with so much rage. "I don't believe my son betrayed me like this after everything I did for his ungrateful ass."

I said, "So, it is true?" I sat in the chair, and Damon sat next to me. The donor whom they call Dad replied, "I don't have to explain myself to anybody, but all I can do is tell you not to be like me. You have every right to hate me for what I did to you." I stared at the ceiling, "is this going anywhere?"

"Shanel, let him talk," said Damon.

I frown, "Well, he needs to hurry up,"

He glanced at Damon, then turned his attention back to me, "It's okay. It's my fault that everything in her life went sour." Said Darren

I replied, "I already know that Darren,"

He asked, "But do you know how?"

I sigh, "No, and please spare me the details, Darren." The nurse comes into the room to take away his food and check his vital signs as we talk.

The donor they call dad, said, "For me to cleanse my heart, I will tell you everything."

I shake my head, "I get it. You want to dump all your burdens on me so I can be a nervous wreck. Are you still trying to destroy me?"

"No, Shanel, that's not what I'm trying to do." Said Darren

I get up from my chair, "Why now? Why dump all this on me when you know damn well, I can't handle any more negative energy from you. Hell, I am finally trying to get my life back on track. I don't need any more drama in my life."

"Shanel, chill and sit down. Stop being stubborn. Just listen to what your dad has to say so you both can move on." Said Damon

Darren chuckles, "You remind me of my sister Charlotte. She was my baby sister, he sighs. My sister has gone to be with the Lord, but Charlotte was one stubborn mule. You could not make her do anything unless she wanted to. Darren laughs. Mama could not get her to wash dishes, cook, or do her hair. She would go to school nappy-headed. The boys used to pick on her every day. She did not care because she was content with herself. Unlike me, I was weak and still am.

I met a woman by the name of Lorraine Weston. She was a fortuneteller. I was 19, and your mom was 18. We thought it would be fun for her to tell us about our future. She said that your mother and I would get married and be happy. As always, there was a catch: our firstborn had to be a boy because he would bring us many blessings. Then Shelly asked what would happen if we had a girl? Lorraine Weston gave us a weary look and told us woe will be unto us for the rest of our lives. She said our family would be cursed and we would never have happiness. That scared the hell out of us. Lorraine saw the fear on our faces. She said we should return to her with $120 if we had a girl, and we agreed. It was a stupid idea; we thought she was in our best interest."

I said, "So, all that crap you wrote about how your boys…" The donor they call dad cut me off, "All lies; I didn't know how to tell you that Shelly and I trusted a fortuneteller with our lives. He sighs; we took you back to Lorraine after you were born. When she saw you, she began chanting over you. She took you from Shelly's arms, walked into this room, and closed the door. We heard you crying. Her chants became louder and louder. Then, she begins to pray in a different language. Shelly became scared. We didn't know what we had gotten ourselves into. Your mother grabbed my hands so tight, and then, suddenly, it was quiet. She opens the door and comes out of the room with you covered in red stuff. Your Mama had this baffled look on her face. She asked Lorraine what is this red stuff on our baby? Lorraine said it was chicken blood. As she handed you back to Shelly, she told your mother and me that we need to sprinkle chicken blood over you once a week so that we are the family and wouldn't be cursed." Tears run down the donor they call dad face, "Two years later, I found out through my sister Darla that Lorraine was a voodoo priestess, and the ritual she performed on you was a reversed spell to benefit her. Lorraine took all your positive energy and gave you her negative karma. That's why you were suffering, going through a hard time."

I asked, "What about you and Shelly?"

Darren sighs, "Well, as long as we kept bringing you back to Lorraine, our life would be good." I was fuming, I asked, "So you let that bitch put a curse on me?" The donor they call Dad wipes the tears from his face. I glared at him with rage, "You kept the curse going on, and you didn't stop it?"

"No, because life was great, Shelly and I had a great paying job,"
I frowned, speaking in anger, "That's why I was suffering, for the love of money. Thanks a lot, Darren. You are a selfish bastard,"

Damon gets up from his chair and walks out of the donor they call dad room in anger; I follow behind him, "Are you okay?"

He replied, "Hell no, I should be asking you, are you okay? Man, if I were still in those streets, he would be a dead man. I'm going to take a walk before I gouge his eyes out or beat the muthafucker to death," I sigh before walking back into the donor they call dad, room. "I understand he's angry with me, but I went to New Orleans. I found somebody who told me how to get rid of the curse and that it would take time to wear off." Said Darren

I frown, "so why did you and my mother want to kill me?"

"That was the curse wearing off," said Darren. I sat back in the chair, 'What do you mean?"

He replied, "Well, the man told me that while the curse is wearing off, it would bring the worst out of Shelly and me, so I shot myself so it wouldn't affect me." Damon walked back into Darren's room handing me bottled water. "Thanks," he sat next to me. Damon is fuming, clutching his jaws, "So let me get this straight, you worked witchcraft on an innocence baby who didn't ask to be in this fucking world."

Darren looks toward Shanel, "I'm sorry. I wish I could take it back," I get up from the chair and walk toward Darren, "but you can't. I'm so through with this family. I won't disown you, but I'm no longer coming around this family. Let me ask you a question. Do you have any ounce of love for me in your heart, Darren?" He looks at me, takes a deep breath, then closes his eyes. Damon asked, "You ready to go, Shanel?"

She replied in frustration, "Yeah, like right now." Darren sighed,

"I hope you can truly forgive me and your mother, Shanel." I frowned at Darren. "I hope you can forgive yourself, Darren." Sharon and Jada entered Darren's room as I reached for my purse. Jada smiled, "What's up, Damon?"

He said, "Hey,"

Sharon smiles, "Hey Shanel, how are you?"

I replied, "I am good."

Sharon's smile fades, "I was hoping we could go to lunch to start our sister's healing process."

I shake my head, "I am going to decline. It would be best if you did your healing. You have a lot going on. You just found out that your mother committed suicide in front of the donor you call daddy. I won't be forced or pretend everything is cool when it's not. I forgive, but I don't forget."

I glanced at Jada. How was the visit with your mother, Ms. Waters?" Jada holds her head down. "Never mind, your body language tells the story." Sharon sighs, "You shouldn't hold me and Jada accountable for what Darren did. It wasn't our fault." "Sharon, are you serious right now? You played right into the devil's hand instead of coming over to my townhouse and treating me like your sister with respect. You two tore me down in my time of need. I don't understand why you attended church; God's people don't tear you down. They help lift you up in Jesus' name."

"But daddy…" I cut Sharon off. "Stop blaming the donor you call daddy for everything. You, Jada, and Melissa have your own mind. You did what you wanted to do, isn't that right, Jada?"

Jada avoids looking at me, "What's wrong, Jada? Cat got your tongue now. You'll need to own up to your mistakes because when judgment day comes, you can't blame anybody but yourself for the road you took. Oh yeah, before I forget, I will not participate in the family counseling. That chapter of my life is closed for good." Sharon cries, "We still have unresolved issues that we need to work out as a family, Shanel,"

I replied, "My issues resolved. I went to the source," they look toward Darren,

Sharon asked, "Well, could you fill us in?"

I said, "My issues don't concern you two. That's between me, Darren, and my mother,"

Jada looks at me with teary eyes, "But we sisters, we can help each other with our issues,"

I frown, "Please, you didn't treat me like a sister; you treated me like an outsider, but it's all good. Alright, I'm out. Take care and be blessed, family." Damon and I walked out of Darren's hospital room. Sharon and Jada step outside Darren's room, watching their sister walk out of their life for good, wiping their tears away. Damon smiled, looking at Shanel walking toward the elevator, "You handle that like a true soldier. I thought you were going to kill Darren's ass."

I smirk, "Trust me, I was sure thinking about it,"

Damon asked, "So what will do about your mama?"

I shrug my shoulder, "There's nothing I can do. She was so far gone that when we were in the meeting, she didn't want to make amends. She was still bashing and blaming me for everything."

"Well, at least one parent mended the fences with you." We get on the elevator.

I frown, "Yeah, it had to take my daddy shooting himself.,"

Damon smiles, "You just called Darren daddy," I smile, "I know, and I didn't say it with anger; I truly forgive him. I am no longer trapped under the devil," Damon and I get off the elevator and leave the hospital.

Chapter 26

Sharon and Jada walk back into Darren's room, wiping their tears away. He is looking at his two daughters, "What do you all want?"

Sharon frowned, "You can calm that attitude down, Daddy. We came to ask you about Melissa," he began to cough. Jada walks out of the room to get him some water. Sharon pulls the chair next to Darren's bed. She glances at the paperwork on his tray, "Hold up, you are being released today instead of Friday?" Jada walks back in with a cup of water. She hands it to Darren. He drinks the cup of water and then hands it back to Jada. "What do you all want to know about Melissa? Well, at the family meeting, she was quiet,"

Darren looks confused, "I don't see a problem with her being quiet. Maybe she didn't have anything to say."

"Well, she left without saying goodbye, and that's not like her." Said, Sharon.

He sighs, looking up at the ceiling, "Well then, you need to ask her, not me."

"No, we're coming to you. Now, what's going on with Melissa?" asked Sharon.

Darren sighs, "Okay, you want the truth. Have a sit before Shelly comes to pick me up." Sharon asked, "Why is she picking you up instead of your wife?"

"Because my wife is going to file for a divorce."

Jada added, "Deborah referred to Daddy as her soon-to-be ex-husband. Girl, I promise you don't pay attention." Sharon chuckles, "You're right. She did say that when she was going off on us." Darren frowns, "My wife participated in the family counseling? Damn, you'll had a field day blasting me out."

Jada replied with an attitude, "We sure did. Let's get back to Melissa." Darren sighs, "She is quiet because she has been fighting her own demons."

Sharon said, "She not going through anything, and if she were, I would be the first to know."

Darren frowned, "Well, did you know she is sleeping with my brother, her daddy, for money." Sharon and Jada's mouths drop to the floor, "You are lying; she is not sleeping with her daddy." Darren smirks, "Well, you can believe me or not, but I know the truth, and I know my brother. That's why her mother disowned her and left my brother. Now I am finished talking."

Sharon shakes her head, "We are not finished, Daddy. Damn! This family is going to burn in hell. There isn't anything Godly about your side of the family, daddy. I just want to know why you didn't tell me my Mama committed suicide in front of you?"

"I'm not going to rehash the past, Sharon." She cries, "You owe me an explanation, Daddy." He laughs, "I don't owe you or anybody else a damn thing. That's the past. You can't change what happens. Take the old folks' advice, stop crying over spilled milk, and get you a new glass."

Sharon shakes her head in disgust, "you don't have any remorse for the things you have done against this family? In Shanel's words, well, the donor we used to call Daddy, you don't have to ever worry about me anymore because you are officially dead to me, you fucking serpent." Jada nodded in agreement, "You take care, Darren." He dismissed his daughters with a wave. "Ya'll not hurting my feeling." He laughed as they left his room. They passed Shelly at the nurse's station without speaking to her. Shelly smirked, mumbling to herself, "Stupid bitches," Sharon and Jada walked to the elevator in deep conversation, "We have one fucked up family. Daddy's side of the family is full of demons. I wish we could trade our daddy for a new one." Said Jada

Sharon frowns, "Well, at least we know what's going on with Melissa. We need to see her. Why would she sleep with her daddy? If she needed money, all she had to do was ask. Hell, I would have hit the strip pole or sold drugs, not slept with my daddy. Shit, I can't take any more secrets from this family."

"That's why I said earlier I was going to cancel our session with Pastor Dobbins and work on ourselves. I don't think we should see Melissa. We need to leave well enough alone. I'm definitely going to call Pastor Dobbins tonight when I get home." Said Jada

Sharon and Jada walk to the car. "We can't cry over our family issues anymore. We need to improve our lives, so if I have to move and leave my family in Atlanta, GA, to better myself, then I will." Said, Sharon.

Jada asked, "What about me?"

She replied, "I love you, but sometimes you have to leave for a change, and that's what I'm going to do. Family will talk about you, put you down, lie, and hurt you the most. We know that all too well because we did that to Shanel." Jada asked, "So you serious about leaving me in Atlanta,"

Sharon replied, "Yes, Jada, I need a change. I can't stay here anymore, knowing how my mother died. I need to get away from this family." Jada's eyes tear up, and asked, "We will keep in contact, right?" Sharon sighs, tears rolling down her face. "I'm going to do what Shanel is doing."

Jada cries, "But we were close. How can you walk away from me?"

Sharon replied, "Jada, it's not easy, but I'm doing what is best for me, and you need to do the same." Sharon hugs her sister before getting in the car. Alright, sis, you take care of yourself," Sharon gets in her car and drives off. "Lord forgive me but I'm still going to stay in Atlanta. I will move to another townhome, maybe closer to my job. Jada gets in the car and calls Ms. Waters "She answers on the second ring, "Hello,"

Jada clears her throat, "Hey Ms. Water, this is Jada. Did you want to go to dinner tomorrow?"

Ms. Waters replied, "Sure, that would be nice,"

Jada smiles, "Okay, okay, I'll pick you up around six." She hangs up with Ms. Waters and calls her cousin Melissa, she answers with a sad tone, "Hey, Jada,"

She asked, "Hey, are you okay?"

She replied, "Yeah, my daddy just left," Jada asked, "So why are you so sad, Melissa?"

She replied, "I'm just going through the motions of life, nothing

I can't handle."

"Well, if you want to talk or need anything, just let me know. I'm just a phone call away, Melissa,"

"Thank you. I appreciate that, Jada. Well, I need to go take a shower. I will talk to you later." Jada shakes her head. "The world we live in—I can't understand it, Lord. I can move on without my daddy and sisters in my life." She deletes her daddy and Sharon's number, "I get it." Jada cranks up her car and leaves the hospital.

Chapter 27

We pulled up in the driveway of my townhome. Josh is walking across the street with Catalina and Terry, "Hey, Mommy," I open the car door, and hug my son. Catalina smiles at me, "Hey Catalina,"

"Hi, may I have a word with you?" My smile fades away. "Damon takes the boys into the house, "What's wrong, Catalina?"

She sighs, "I lost my job two weeks before you moved in. I was using my rainy-day funds until I found another job. Well, my funds are almost depleted, so Terry and I are moving to Florida to stay with my sister."

I hug her, "I am so sorry; Josh is going to be so sad." Catalina smiles, "I know the boys were just starting to form a brotherly bond."

"Well, if there's anything that Damon and I can do, just let us know."

She hugs me again, "Thank you, Shanel, but my sister is taking care of everything for me."

I began sweating. "Girl, it's hot out here; let's go inside and get something to drink." I open the front door. We walk to the kitchen and see the boys eating an ice cream sandwich at the kitchen table. I open the refrigerator, "What do you want to drink Catalina?"

"I'll take whatever you have. I'm not a picky person."

I replied, "I have a white grape pineapple mix drink,"

Catalina smiled, "That's fine," I placed her drink on the table, "Thank you, you have an awesome home,"

I smiled "Thank you,

Damon came downstairs, "What are you two up to? "We are just talking, where are you headed to?" I asked.

"I need to go visit my mom. I should be back in an hour." Said Damon

Catalina said, "Terry and I need to be heading out. We have a busy day ahead of us." Terry hugs Josh, "I'll see you tomorrow."

Damon said, "I'll walk y'all to the door since I'm on my way out anyway." I finish drinking my juice and follow my son into the family room to watch TV. I asked, "Are you happy, Josh?"

He replied, "Yes, Mommy, I like staying here even though Terry and his mommy are moving away." I frown, "who told you?"

"Terry said he overheard his mommy talking on the phone to his auntie that his daddy isn't coming back home anymore. I'm going to miss Terry. He is my best friend in the whole wide world." I smiled at my son. The front door opened, and I jumped off that sofa quickly. Damon walked into the family room. "Man, you scared the hell out of me. What are you doing back here?"

He chuckles, "I was talking to my Mama on the phone. Her ass is out on a date with some dude name Mario. They have been dating for almost a year. She failed to inform me about this information." I chuckle, "Your mama is a grown woman. She doesn't need your permission." Damon frowns, shaking his head. "I know that. I'm just concerned. I don't know anything about Mario. He better have his own money, house, and car. These sorry-ass men nowadays don't want to work. They want to live off the woman." I chuckle, "chill the hell out."

Josh asked, "Daddy, can we build a forte tonight?"

Damon smiles, "Sure, little man,"

I said, "Can you make sure Josh goes to bed on time?"

He replied, "Okay," I walked upstairs to my bedroom and closed the door. I go into my bathroom to run a lukewarm tub bath with bubbles. I get my clothes together before returning to the bathroom to enjoy my relaxing bath time. In the meantime, Damon is curious to know what Shanel is doing. He walks upstairs to Shanel's bedroom and calls her name, "Shanel, Shanel," she doesn't answer, and he panics. Damon enters the bathroom and sees Shanel in the tub with her eyes closed. He sprinkles water on her face, and she wakes up, "What the hell!"

"My bad," said Damon.

I asked, "What are you doing in my bathroom? And where is Josh?"

He said, "Calm down, He is watching TV. Are you okay?"

I sigh, "Yes, I just need to relax." Damon smiles at me, "You want me to give you a sponge bath?"

I replied, "I can sponge my own body. You just need to leave so I can continue to relax. Bye, Damon."

"I just want to say one thing: you look beautiful with no make-up and your hair pinned up." I blushed, "Thank you, Damon. Now leave, please,"

"Okay, I'm leaving, girl. Your beauty is killing me," I continue blushing. "Lord, he just made my night," he smiles as he closes the bathroom door. I begin having a conversation with the Lord, "Lord, I just want to thank you for letting me be able to face my daddy. I no longer have hate in my heart for him, but I do feel sorry for him. I may not be perfect, but I'm trying my best, Lord. I must work on forgiving all my family members, but it is hard, Lord. They have done a lot of evil things to me. I don't want to hold grudges for the rest of my life. I want to be free Jesus from the shackles that hold me down. I want to be free Jesus from the curses that people have spoken against me. I want to be free Jesus from the iniquity that surrounds my atmosphere. I want to be free in the name of Jesus." I began bathing myself, removing all the filthy sins that corroded my body. I let the water out of the tub and then jumped into the shower to rinse my body. I got out the shower, "lords it's been a long time since I was able to soak in the tub and not worry about roaches trying to crawl in my bath water, I'm so grateful for that." I dry off, then spray my body with lavender and peppermint spray. I put my clothes on and walked into my bedroom to read my bible. In the meantime, Josh and his daddy are having fun making a forte in the middle of the family room for them to sleep underneath tonight. Damon and his son go upstairs to get pillows and cover to complete their forte. I leave my bedroom, "What are you two up to?" Josh begins talking with excitement, "Me and Daddy build a forte in the middle of the living room."

I smile, "Is that so?" Damon nods in agreement, "Yes, ma'am, come downstairs Mommy and see what we built." I followed them downstairs, "On my goodness. Your forte is huge."

Josh asked, "You like it, Mommy?"

"Yes baby, well, you and your daddy have fun. I'm going to bed," Josh kissed me on the cheek. "Good night, Mommy,"

Damon asked, "Do I get to kiss you on the cheek good night, too?" before I could respond, Josh said, "Yeah, let Daddy kiss you on the cheek, Mommy." I frowned, "No, he's too old for that, baby." Josh frowned, "Okay," Damon walked up to me as Josh went into his forte. I smirked as he leaned in and kissed my cheek softly, and my smirk turned into a smile. "Good night, Shanel," I trip on my way going to the stairs. "Are you okay?" I ran upstairs without responding and closed my room door. Damon smiled, shaking his head and joining his son underneath the forte. "I promise that man makes me tingle every time," I lay in my bed smiling.

Chapter 28

Damon is sitting on Shanel's bed, watching her sleep. She let out a large fart, Damon jumped out of bed, waking her up, "damn girl, you let a big ball of gas out your ass," I laughed as Damon sprayed my peppermint and lavender body spray. I asked, "Why are you in my room anyway?"

He said, "I came to see if your ass was still alive. It's after ten a.m., and Josh has already left for school. I just wanted to talk to you about my plans."
I asked, "Can I brush my teeth first?"

Damon replied, "No, this is important, so you know I was supposed to leave after my cousin Dee's funeral, but due to current events, I'm going cut my time short and leave tomorrow." I hold my head down, "Don't worry I will ensure you and Josh are well taken care of. I'm going to have a real estate agent look for a house for my mama,"

I smile, "Hey, I was thinking."

He asked, "About what?"

"Why not give your mama this townhome,"

He shakes his head, "Nah, I will get her a new townhome,"

"Oh, my goodness, Damon, just give your mom this townhome. Josh and I can move to California with you."

Damon smiled, "Are you serious? You really want to move to

California with me?"

"Yeah, Josh and I need a change," Damon smiles, "Look, I have a few errands to do. I'll be back in time to pick up Josh."

I sat on the side of the bed, "I think I just made a mistake. If Damon wanted me to go to California, he would have asked me. I get up from the bed and walk to the dresser to get my phone. I dial Damon's number, and he picks up on the second ring, "what's up,"

"Um, I wasn't thinking right this morning. I rush into a decision: I'm going to pass on the move to California."

Damon's voice cracks, "Why?"

I replied, "I think it's best for me and Josh,"

"Let me talk to you when I return home." Damon hangs up and calls Ms. Waters, "hello,"

"Ms. Waters, this is Damon. Are you up for company?" she sighs, "What's wrong?"

He replied, "I need some advice,"

"Hell, I can advise over the phone—no need to waste gas. Now, what's on your mind?" asked Ms. Waters. Damon pulled into the gas station, parking his BMW beside the free air pump. He replied, "Do you think if I ask Shanel to marry…" Ms. Waters began coughing. "Did I hear you right? You want to marry Shanel?"

He replied, "Yeah, she still has my heart; Shanel is my tender roni that Bobby Brown be singing about,"

"So why do you need my advice? Damon, you already know what you want to do." Said Ms. Waters.

Damon replied, "You make it sound so easy."

She said, "Damon, stop being a damn coward. If you love Shanel, then you ask her and stop wasting my damn time."

Damon chuckles, "Why are you so harsh to me?"

Ms. Waters chuckles, "Because you are a man, not a little boy, you don't need my advice. Your heart is all the advice you need. Just follow it. You know how you want your future to go, Damon. Now get your ass off the phone and handle your business."

He said, "Yes 'ma," Damon chuckles as he gets off the phone, "I'm going to miss that crazy ass woman," he sits in his car thinking about how he's going to approach Shanel. "Lord, I don't usually ask you for anything, but I need your help to propose to Shanel. You know she can be sweet and harsh. I need you to touch her heart toward me and accept my proposal. I love that girl. She gave birth to my son, who means the world to me. I want to make it official, Lord." Damon calls his friend in California, "What up, are you on your way back to Cali Ace?"

He chuckles, "I'm trying, Ace. I'm about to propose to the mother of my child."

"Aiight, handle that, Ace, and get your ass back to Cali. I have two artists that I may want to sign to my label. I want to see what you think before I invest my muthafucking money."

Damon chuckles, "I got you, D-Man, but real talk, Ace. Did you get nervous when you proposed to your girl?"

"Ace, I was sweating like a muthafucker. I had diarrhea. My ass was shook." Damon laughs, "Damn, Ace, you had it bad."

He replied, "Yeah, I did, but I married the love of my life, my heart, and my best friend. We have been married for twelve years. I wouldn't trade my wife for any of these thirsty broads. She got my love for life."

"I hear that, aiight D-Man, I'm going to get with you later," he hangs up the phone, a hand gently taps on his window. An older lady has her right on her hip, speaking loudly with frustration, "Excuse me, I have been waiting ten minutes to use the air pump. Can you kindly move your damn car out of the way before my tire goes flat?" Damon chuckles, "My bad," he backs out and drives off, getting on Highway 92. He gets stopped by the red light. Damon glances to the right and sees Gina trying to get his attention. He rolls his window down, "what's up?"

She smiles, "Pullover in the next plaza. We need to talk."

"Aiight," When the light turns green, he drives to the plaza and parks. Gina pulls up on the side of him. She gets out of her car, and Damon unlocks his door so she can get inside. "You know I am mad at you, right?" He laughs, "Why are you mad, Gina?"

She replied, "Why haven't you been over to my place?" He rubs his head, then turns to Gina, "I have a lot on my plate right now."

She said, "I heard about your cousin, man that was crazy how he got killed across the street from me. I still can't believe that shit. So, when is the funeral?"

Damon cleared his throat, trying to fight back his tears, "My auntie dumb ass cremated him and flushed his ashes down the fucking toilet. That some hateful shit; she lucky she my mama sister."

Gina frowns, "Calm down, it's going to be all right. Karma will find her." Gina turns to Damon, grabbing his hand, "I love you, Damon. I'm going to divorce my husband so we can be together. You don't have to worry about Shanel. She has moved out." Damon looks confused, slowly pulling his hand away from Gina. "What the hell are you talking about? You are my fucking homegirl."

She said, "Damon, please don't act like there's nothing between us. We slept together three times when my husband was out of town visiting his shady ass family."

He scoffed, "I remember, that's the night Shanel's mama told me she was messing with my friend, which was a lie."

She frowns, "So I was a fucking rebound. I sucked your dick and let you cum in my mouth Damon." She begins to cry, "Why?" He sighs, "Stop crying, Gina. You knew from the jump that I love Shanel. I told you that the night when we had sex. You chose to come on to me and suck my dick." Gina wiped away her tears, "So why did you have sex with me, Damon?"

He replied, "Shit, you suck my dick, then rub it against your wet pussy. I wasn't going to turn down no free pussy." She frowns, "Well, at least I know where we stand. Does Shanel know you fucked me raw?"

Damon replied, "Yep, Ms. Waters already told her?"

Gina frown asking, "How the hell does her nosy ass know about us?"

"I tell her everything," Damon phone rings, he picks up on the first ring, "What's up, mama?"

She asked, "Where you at?"

He said, "I am in the car talking to Gina. What you need, mama?"

She asked, "Can you bring my grandson over to the house? I have something for him."

He replied, "Yeah, I can do that?"

"Do you think Shanel will let Josh spend the night so he can go to church with me? I'm trying to do right by my grandchild; life is too short."

Damon smiled, "I don't see why not."

She said, "Okay, will you ask her for me, Damon?"

"I got you, mama." Damon hangs up with his mama. Gina asked, "Damon, do you think we would have been together if we had met first?"

He chuckles, "Hell nah, you more like a homegirl to kick it with."
She asked in a soft voice, "Is it because I'm fat?"

Damon was firm, "Hell nah, you a fucking cheater. You have been cheating on your husband since y'all been married."

She sighed, "I wouldn't cheat on you, Damon, you the kind man that I that will do right by. You fine as hell, brown-skinned, nicely built with a big dick, and you take care of your son. I need you in my life, Damon. Can I be your side chick?"

He gets annoyed, "Gina, get out of my car. I'm done with you, shorty."

She begs, "Can I please suck your dick?" Damon shouts, "Get the fuck out of my car. What the hell is wrong with you?" Gina slowly gets out of the car as Shanel's sister comes out of the store. "Hey Jada," she walks over to Gina, "Hey girl, what are you doing here?"

Gina smirks, "I was talking to Damon," he gets out of his car, "Hey Jada, why are you two over in the cut talking to each other." Gina continued smirking, "We were talking about the night we had sex?" Damon was caught off guard, "Bitch! What the fuck did you just say?" Gina got in her car quickly so Damon wouldn't come after her. Jada threw her bags at Damon, "That's why you be over that whore house all the time. You don't love my sister, you lying ass dog." Gina is sitting in her car laughing. Jada walks off, trying to call her sister, and she picks up, "Shanel, don't hang up. Damon is cheating on you with Gina?" Damon shouts, "Not true!"

"It is Shanel. They are in the parking lot, and the bitch just said they were talking about the night they had sex."

Shanel asked, "Jada, where are you?"

She replied, "Off Highway 92 by the plaza next to the high school you attended in Roswell."

"Okay, thanks, Jada. Put him on the phone." She hands Damon the phone. I take a deep breath. "Shanel, listen to me."
She cut him off, "Damon, what's going on?"

He replied in anger, "Gina is trying to start shit. She is sitting in her car laughing." He walks away from Jada, "Shanel, I didn't sleep with that girl again."

"Damon, I'm not mad. I'm not your girlfriend. You don't have to explain anything to me. It's good that you are leaving tomorrow." Damon asked, "Shanel, do you believe me?"

I replied, "Damon, I'm good?"

He said, "I didn't ask you that. I asked you if you believe me?"

I sigh, heavily through the phone, "Damon, let's just drop this conversation." He walks toward Jada, handing her the phone. She shakes her head, "Hello, are you okay, sis?"

"I'm good, Jada. Let me get off this phone. I need to finish doing me?"

Jada said, "You take care, Shanel."

"You too, Jada." Damon walks to his car and cranks it up. He glances at Gina and then pulls out his parking space, speeding off. Jada walks over to Gina. She rolls down her window."

"How long have you been sleeping with my sister's man?"

Gina frowns, "Damon is not dating Shanel,"

Jada chuckles, "Yes, he is. You need to be worried about your own man and get off my sister's man. He doesn't want your nasty fat ass." Gina chuckles, "Honey, let me school you. We fucked raw. Trust me, he's not dating Shanel." Gina rolled up her window, smirking. Jada spit on her car as she backed out of the parking lot. Jada walks back to her car, "Damn, I have to replace my groceries." She walks back into the store.

Chapter 29

Damon drove to Ms. Waters' townhouse in anger. He parked his car. He got out of his car, pulled this phone out of his pocket, and called Ms. Waters, "Hey, Ms. Waters, can you come outside? I need to talk to you." She came outside smoking her weed. "What's wrong, Damon?"

"Ms. Waters, my day was going good until I bumped into Gina; I fucked up any chances with Shanel." Ms. Waters shakes her head. "I told you she was no good." Damon paused. Ms. Waters was puzzled, she asked, "What's wrong, Damon?"

He replied, "Shanel is pissed off with me. I was on my way to buy her an engagement ring. She is not going to let me in the house."

"Let me talk to her, Gina's husband comes outside, waving at Damon and Ms. Waters. He walks across the street. "Why the hell is he coming over here for?" asked Ms. Waters. "Hey y'all, man, where have you been?"

Damon replied, "Trying to handle business,"

Ray-Ray said, "Man, my wife has been upset with you." Ms. Waters chuckles, "Why she already has a husband."

Ray-Ray chuckles, "Ms. Waters, chill out with that. My wife loves me. Gina and Damon have a special bond; they are like brothers and sisters." Ms. Water continues puffing on her weed. Gina pulls up to her townhouse. She gets out of the car and calls her husband. "Ray-Ray, can you come here, please? Damon glanced in her direction, "Um, before you go Ray-Ray, you need to talk to all your boys that be at your house." he gave Damon that fighting look, "Your wife has been sucking dicks for a year, hell she even sucked my mines when I was drunk." He shuns Damon off, "Man, is that all Gina probably fucked the entire hood. I thought you were going to say she was spending my money on another dude or having a baby. He chuckles, I'll catch up with you later, Damon."

"Yeah, later," Ms. Waters laughs, "Lord, those demons belong together. You go back to Shanel while I talk to her on the phone." He hugs Ms. Water, "thanks," Damon smiles getting back into his car, and backs out the driveway. He speeds off not looking in Gina direction, she frowns as he passes by. Her husband slaps her on the butt, "You know what I want," she rolls her eyes at him, "Let's go."

Ms. Waters walks back into her townhouse, and calls Shanel, "Hey Ms. Waters, what's up?"

"Damon just left my house. He was angry. You know Gina is full of shit, Damon didn't sleep with that girl again. She's just mad that you and Damon are getting back together."

"Ms. Waters, I'm not mad with Damon. Knowing that Gina was in his presence, I didn't want to talk about it over the phone. We are not dating. He's just helping me get back on my feet." She coughs, "Damn, I puff that hard. Look, Shanel, the devil is attacking you all in relationship, so don't give Damon a hard time, all right."

I replied, "Yes, ma'am. He should be home soon." My phone beeped, "Hold on, Ms. Waters, this Damon."

"No, no, you go ahead and talk to him," said Ms. Waters

"Okay, talk to you later," she clicked on the other line, "Hello," Damon's voice was low, "I'm going to pick up Josh. Is it okay if I take him over to my mama's house for the night?"

I was shocked, "Really, your mama wants to spend time with Josh?"

He replied, "yeah,"

I smile, "Okay, I'll get his clothes together,"

"Don't worry about it. I'll take him to the mall to get some clothes,"

I asked, "Well, can I at least see my son before he leaves for the night?"

"I'll bring him by,"

"Thanks, Damon." I walk upstairs, talking to myself. I can't believe Damon's mama wants to spend time with her grandson. Things are changing for the better. I smile, lying across the bed. I call my sister Jada, "Hello, Shanel,"

"Hey Jada, what are you doing?" she replied, "I'm just getting home from the store and about to cook something to eat."

She chuckles, "I didn't know you knew how to cook. Your ass is always dining out with Sharon."

"Whatever I can cook, Shanel,"

"Okay, anyway, I just want to thank you for having my back, Jada."

"That's what sisters are for Shanel. Speaking of sisters, Sharon said that she's leaving Atlanta for good."

I said, "Sometimes you have to move away to start over and be happy,"

"I guess, did you and Damon get everything situated?" asked Jada.

I sigh, "Yeah, Gina has always liked Damon. She was trying to start crap as usual." Josh comes running upstairs, "I'm going to talk to you later," She hangs up with Jada and gives Josh a huge hug. "I just came in to see you before I go to granny's house."

I said, "Okay, where is your daddy?"

"He's in the car," said Josh.

"You have fun, baby,"

"Mama, I am having so much fun. Are you having fun, mama?" I smiled at Josh. "Yes, baby, now give me another hug." I walked downstairs with Josh, walking him to the front door. I watched him walk to his daddy's car. Damon glanced at me. I closed the door, walked back upstairs, and lay across the bed to nap.

Chapter 30

I wake up in a pitch-dark bedroom. I cut on the lights. I scratched my head, looking at the clock on my nightstand. It's ten o'clock. I turn on the hallway lights and walk downstairs. I walk into the family room. I see the back door is open. Damon is sitting outside smoking weed. I joined him on the patio deck and sat in silence. He got up after his weed was done and walked back inside the house, not saying a word to me. I propped my feet in the other chair, enjoying the summer night. Damon comes back outside and I hear Jazz playing outside. He turns on the outside lights. I am blown away by how he tried to decorate the small backyard with roses and white lights. Damon sat across from me, looking at my expression. He didn't smile. He just watched me. "What is this all about, Damon, "Well, I was going to ask you to be my wife, but after all that shit, jump down early today with Gina. I was like fuck it, so it's no use wasting the decorations, right? So, I'll let you enjoy since you are outside on the deck." I look around, "Well, it looks nice, Damon." He stares at me, "What, Damon?"

He frowned, "I thought you really knew me; how could you think I would sleep with Gina again?"

I yawned, "I don't want to talk about that. I just woke up from a peaceful sleep." He walks back into the house. I got up from the table and walked inside the house. I walk back upstairs to my bedroom and close the door. I saw a gold bag on the bed. I didn't bother to open it; I frowned, tossing it to the side. I flop on my bed, lying down. Damon walks into the room, "Why didn't you look in the bag?"

"I just didn't. Can you leave out my room?" Damon finishes smoking his weed. He grabs me out of bed, "Stop, Damon! What the hell are you doing? Put me down, Damon!" He picked me up over his shoulder, grabbed the gold bag, and walked back downstairs. He sat me back outside on the patio deck. Damon sat across from her, "Open the bag, Shanel?"

I asked, "Why?"

"Just open the bag, Sheesh!" I sighed, looking at the bag, and then looked inside. It was a big white box. "it's really light," I opened the box. It was a picture of me and Damon on our first date. I smiled, "I remember this, that was so long ago. You kept all the good pictures." Damon eyes are glazing at me. He asked, "Do you love me?"

I replied, "The question is, do you love me?"

He said, "Hell yeah, I love you. Do you love me?" I get up from the table and walk into my small, decorated backyard. "I do love you, but it's not going to work out with us. I would rather co-parent with you like you said before. Trust me, once you move to Cali, those groupies are going to be lining up one by one." He gets up from the table and walks toward me. "Damn girl, I'm not worried about them. I want you always to be my one and only. I want to give you my heart, my love, my wealth, and whatever else you want. I'm in love with you, and I'm going to take care of you and Josh." Damon takes the box out of his pocket, "Shanel Nicole Howard, "Will you marry me?" I looked at the ring, "That's a huge diamond. Can you downsize that for me?"

He raised his voice, "What the hell? This is a three-karat ring." I smile, "Thanks, but it's too flashy for me, Damon."

He said, "Girl, you going to wear this ring? Now, what is your answer to my question?"

I asked, "Can I at least take some of the karat from my ring to make earrings?"
He said, "Alright,"

I smile, "Then yes, I will marry you."

Damon asked, "Can we seal the deal with a kiss?" Damon planted his lips on my soft, thick lips, kissing me passionately. "I pull away, "Okay, Damon,"

He chuckles "What?"

I replied, "Can we just chill for a minute? My body is doing some weird things right now." He laughs, "Like what?"

I smile, "Can we just go inside and chill to some jazz?"

"Yeah," Damon cuts the lights off outside, closing the door behind him. I am sitting on the sofa. He turns off the lights in the house, "he turns on the TV to music choices, listening to jazz. I asked, "So, are you still leaving tomorrow?"

Damon said, "Yeah, I am, but I'll be back to get you and Josh." Damon's phone rings; I ask, "Why is it every time we try and chill, your phone starts going off?" he answers, "Hello, Damon, this is Jada. Is my sister with you?" he passes the phone to me, "hello,"

"Hey Shanel,"

"Jada, what's up?"

She said, "Daryl is not doing well. He was asking for you. His life is spiraling downward."

I asked, "Okay, why is he asking for me?"

Jada replied, "He can relate to you."

I asked, "Where is Daryl now?"

Jada replied, "He's at home with his mama. You know daddy and your mama are back together."

I frown, "Not my concern. Well, I guess I'll call him." She hangs up with her sister. Damon props my legs on his lap and gently massages my thighs. "what's wrong?"

I sigh, "Daryl is having a moment. He wants me to call him."

He said, "Right now?"

I replied, "Yes, I need to go upstairs and get my phone."

Damon said, "You stay, I'll get your phone." He rushed upstairs, then ran back, handing me my phone. "He sat back down, picked up where he left off, and massaged my thighs. I looked through my phone to find his number. I dial his number, The phone rings, and he answers on the second ring, "Hello,"

"Hey Daryl, how are you feeling?" his voice gets lower, "can I come stay with you?"

I was shocked, I glance at Damon, "Uh, Daryl, what's wrong with you staying with your mama?"

He replied in a sad tone, "She's not my mama, and I went to go meet my biological mama. She is a fucken bitch. I see why she and

Daddy had a five-year fuck fest. They act just alike." I sigh, "First off, you need to respect Deborah for raising you as her own child. That woman loves you. Forget about your biological mama. Now, you need to focus on finishing college and do whatever makes Daryl happy."

His voice cracks, "I hear what you're saying, but it's not fair. Life keeps dragging us down."

I said, "Look at it like this: God has a major blessing with your name. I need to take my own advice." He chuckles, "Oh, you know daddy kicked me and my mama out the house."

I shake my head, "No, I didn't. Where are you all staying now?"

Daryl sighed, "Ten minutes away from your old job, they have nice apartments. It's in a gated community, so Daddy can't just come over as he pleases." Damon begins massaging my feet, "Daryl, if you need to talk, you know you can call me."

He said, "Did you know that Jada canceled our meeting on Friday with Pastor Dobbins?"

I sigh, "I can see why,"

"We were born into an evil family with so many damn secrets. According to Daddy's sister, we just removed the icing off the cake. We haven't even dug into the cake yet." Said Daryl

I scoff, "Uh, I don't even want to know any more crap about Daddy's family. I'm starting to think that Daddy is really the devil's son." He chuckles, "Sis, I just realized you haven't called Daddy the donor since we have been on the phone."

I said, "You're right. I can't let Daddy keep controlling me. I forgive him, and you need to do the same with Deborah and First Lady Dobbins,"

He said, "I will, you know I was going to expose her in church, but I changed my mind. I'm going to let God deal with her and Daddy. Sis, as always, it's a pleasure talking to you. Love you to life."

"Love you too," Damon took my phone away from me and sat it on the glass table, "Girl, I love you, but I need to address the situation that happened today." I got up from the sofa and sat on Damon's lap, "Uh, you know you're sitting on Big D; you about to wake him up." I chuckle, looking into his eyes, "You don't have to address anything. I know what kind of man I have." He began gently rubbing the middle of my back, "Tell me what kind of man you got." I kissed him on the forehead, "A patient man who will not try to have sex with me tonight." He laughed, "Well, you need to get off my lap before I have you bouncing up and down." I kissed him again, but this time, I planted one on his moist lips; he said, "Stop, you're not playing fair." I kissed him on the neck, "Baby, please stop, you are waking Big D up." I stopped kissing him and let my tongue take over. Damon softly whispered in my ear, "Do you really want to do this?" I paused, looking into Damon's eyes. I hug him. "You truly love me?"

He said, "Yes, that's why I think Gina did her little shenanigans to fuck up our relationship. You got my heart for life."

I chuckle, "When you utter sweet words like that, you make me want to wake up Big D." He laughs, "So what do you want to do now?"

I replied, "Can I just sit on your lap and enjoy the moment?"

Damon smiles, "What you mean is torture me and enjoy sitting on Big D," I chuckle, "What's next for us?"

He sighed rubbing my leg, "Well, when I leave tomorrow night for Cali, I'm going to find a church for us to attend so our son will have a strong foundation. I'm going to purchase a home so you can furnish it however you like. Then I will find a private school for Josh, and everything else will be left up to you to plan the wedding of your dreams."

I smile, "That's my kind of plan. So, do you think your mama will want to move into this townhome?"

Damon said, "Hell yeah! I'm going to give her my BMW, too. I can always buy another car with the money I will be making. So, how do you feel about everything?" I kissed him again before replying, "Happy and nervous. I want everything to go right for us, Damon."

He sighs, "It will. I gave you my heart," I take his hand and place it over my heart, "You have mine, too." He let it stay there, "I'm not going to worry about my family anymore or let the past keep me in bondage. God has brought me through the fire, and I thank him for everything. It was a hard road. I wasn't happy; I was always in tears and pain, but I made it in Jesus' name. I don't know what God's plan is for us, but I will embrace the good and bad." My phone rings, and Damon answers my phone, "What's up, Jada? I need to talk to my sister, please." He passes me the phone, "Hey, Jada,"

She said, "I don't mean to call you so late at night, but you need to get to the hospital." I slid off Damon's lap onto the sofa, "Melissa is in the hospital," I ask, "What happened? Who told you that."

Jada replied, "The hospital called her next of kin, which is me. She tried to take her own life?" I froze in my tracks, "Why would she do that?" Jada sighs, "I will fill you in at the hospital."

I frown, "No, Jada, tell me now,"

Jada clears her throat, "she has been sleeping with her daddy to get money so she can keep up her lavish lifestyle. She got fed up and just snapped."

I turn to Damon with my mouth open, "What the hell did you just say, Jada?"

She said, "You heard me loud and clear."

I'm shocked, "Damn, okay, I'll be there." I hung up with my sister, "We have to go to the hospital. Melissa attempted to kill herself." Damon shakes his head, "damn, your family is on a suicide mission. What the hell is going on? They need to be dipped in the blood of Jesus. What made her want to try and take her own life?"

I sigh, shaking my head, "Brace yourself; she has been having sex with her daddy for money. Now that explains why she was so quiet at the family counseling." Damon gets up from the sofa and grabs my arm. He said, "Before you go, do you see how God is revealing everything to you? Everything you thought was good is crumbling down."

I nodded in agreement, "I see, The devil had me thinking that Jada, Sharon, and Melissa were living the good life," Damon shook his head, "It came with a price." My phone rings: I answer on the first ring, "Hello," Jada is crying on the phone, "She gone," I drop the phone and turn to Damon. He walks toward me to comfort me with a hug. I cry, "Why did she have to die instead of my daddy? I don't understand why he gets to live. He is evil. Damon sat beside me on the sofa. As he picks up my phone off the floor, Jada is still on the phone, crying. "Jada, Jada calm down,"

She cries, "Damon, I have lost my cousin, her daddy, and our daddy should be dead, not her." Damon sighs heavily on the phone, "Life is not fair, Jada." She continued crying on the phone. Damon sat next to me, wrapping his left around me while holding the phone in his right hand. "I'm so tired of my daddy and his evil demonic family secrets. I can't deal with this shit no more; I need a start fresh." Damon hands the phone back to me, "Jada, I heard you talking about a fresh start. What about your mama?"

Jada replied, "My mama and I have dinner plans tomorrow night. I realize that she's the mother who gave birth to me, and Daddy took that away from her. Shanel, I have disrespected her on numerous occasions. Life is short, and I'm going to make the best of our time together before she departs from me with cancer." I smile with tears. "I am happy for you too."

Jada asked, "Did you tell Damon anything about the family counseling?" I said, "No,"

She said, "Thanks, as far as Melissa goes, I think she's going to be cremated. Her mama left years ago when she found out what Melissa and her husband were doing. I don't think she has a will; the only person that's left to take care of her burial is her daddy, Uncle Joseph, and you know he's not going to do right by her."

I sigh deeply, "It's just best not to attend. I'll just remember the good times we had when we were kids." Jada sniffles on the phone, "I'm hanging up. Good night, Shanel." I turn to Damon with tears, "Now can we relax?" he smiles, "yeah," he pecks me on the cheek.

"My family is bleeding pain." Damon nodded in agreement; I turned to him. "Thank you for not giving up on me for being bitter. I know it wasn't easy dealing with me. Damon pecks me on the forehead; I ask, "Can I be honest with you?"

He said, "Yeah,"

I smile, "Off topic, I have to say I miss your braids. They made you look sexy." He chuckles, "So I'm not sexy with my low fad?"

I giggled, "You look all right." He turned off the TV and plugged his phone into the Bluetooth speaker. We chilled on the sofa for the rest of the night, listening to Boney James serenade us.

Chapter 31

I woke up on the sofa by myself. I got up from the sofa and called out for Damon. He didn't answer, so I walked to the front door to see if his car was parked in the driveway. "Where is he?"

I called his phone, and he answered on the first ring, "Where are you?"

"I'm on my way back. I had to pick up Josh. They called my mama in to work on her day off. You know she was not going to pass up no money for anybody. Do you need anything while I'm out?"

I replied, "No, I'm good,"

"Okay, I'll be there in a few." I go upstairs to my bedroom, close the door, and reach for my Bible off the dresser. I begin reading my Bible with so much joy. I lift her hands to the heavens and say, "Thank you, Jesus. I know I have been difficult, and I ask you to forgive me. Jesus, my heart is heavy over the death of my cousin Melissa. Our last words weren't the best, now she's gone. Geesh, life is too short to hold a grudge against my family. Thank you for sparing my life and watching over me and Josh during our difficult time. I praise you, Jesus, for also giving Damon and me a second chance to get it right. I'm glad we can take care of our son together. I want to thank you, Jesus, for letting me be able to close the door on the past and open a new door to a brighter future with you, Jesus. I ask that you help the rest of my family overcome their deep-rooted issues so they, too, can move on and enjoy their life." As I finished my praise, Damon and Josh opened the front door. I come out of my bedroom and walk downstairs. Josh runs toward me when I reach the bottom of the stairs. "Hey, mama," he hugs me, "Look what Grandma bought me." I look inside the bags. "Good lord, she went on a shopping spree?"

"Mama, I have my own Bible, it's blue." I smiled, "I even bought you a shirt,"

"Thank you, Josh, I love it. I will wear my beautiful shirt tomorrow." Damon walks to the family room, flopping on the sofa watching his family. "Damon, did you tell Josh the good news?" he smiles, "Not yet, Josh, come here. I need to tell you something." He runs to his daddy, "Yes sir,"

"Your mama and I are getting married." Josh frowns, "why?"

Damon asked, "What do you mean why?"

He replied, "You and Mama fussed too much when we stayed at the old house. I want my mama to be happy. You promise not to hurt her? God doesn't want to see my mama cry anymore."

Damon and I were shocked, "Lil Man, I love your mama. I will not hurt your mama, my soon-to-be wife. I gave your mama my heart, and she gave me hers." Josh smiled, "Okay, daddy, you can marry mama. Can we watch a movie together? They were interrupted by the doorbell, "I'll get it," said Damon," he walked to open the door, "Hi Damon,"

"Hey Catalina, hey Terry, come on in." He closed the door, and they followed him into the family room. Terry ran toward Josh. He got off the sofa and hugged his best friend. I smiled, "What brings you guys over today?" Catalina's smile faded away, "Terry wanted to spend his last day with Josh. We are leaving tomorrow. Terry wants to go eat pizza and then go to the movies."

"Hey, why don't we all go? Damon is leaving for California tomorrow." Catalina looks confused. "Are you moving to California?"
He replied, "Yeah, I have a great job waiting for me." Catalina smiled, "Congratulations, Damon. Are you and Josh going to be here by yourself?"

I replied, "Only for two weeks. Josh and I are moving to California with Damon."

He smiles, "Yeah, she has a wedding to plan." Catalina walks over to hug me. "Congrats, do not forget my invitation. I will give you my sister's information. Now, let's celebrate. I am driving said Catalina."

I said, "Okay, let me get ready." Damon and Catalina watch TV with the kids, waiting for me to come downstairs. I came down twenty minutes later. "I'm ready, guys." Catalina smiled. "All right, let's celebrate new beginnings." Damon and I smile, looking at each other. He leans toward me, giving me a soft peek on the lips, "Girl, I love you so much," I chuckle. "I know," they walk out the front door laughing.